Seeing with Poetic Eyes

BREAKTHROUGHS IN THE SOCIOLOGY OF EDUCATION

Series Editors:

George W. Noblit, *University of North Carolina at Chapel Hill*

Joseph R. Neikirk *Distinguished Professor of Sociology of Education University of North Carolina at Chapel Hill*

In this series, we are establishing a new tradition in the sociology of education. Like many fields, the sociology of education has largely assumed that the field develops through the steady accumulation of studies. Thomas Kuhn referred to this as 'normal science.' Yet normal science builds on a paradigm shift, elaborating and expanding the paradigm. What has received less attention are the works that contribute to paradigm shifts themselves. To remedy this, we will focus on books that move the field in dramatic and recognizable ways—what can be called breakthroughs.

Kuhn was analyzing natural science and was been less sure his ideas fit the social sciences. Yet it is likely that the social sciences are more subject to paradigm shifts than the natural sciences because the social sciences are fed back into the social world. Thus sociology and social life react to each other, and are less able separate the knower from the known. With reactivity of culture and knowledge, the social sciences follow a more complex process than that of natural science. This is clearly the case with the sociology of education. The multiplicity of theories and methods mix with issues of normativity— in terms of what constitutes good research, policy and/or practice. Moreover, the sociology of education is increasingly global in its reach—meaning that the national interests are now less defining of the field and more interrogative of what is important to know. This makes the sociology of education even more complex and multiple in its paradigm configurations. The result is both that there is less shared agreement on the social facts of education but more vibrancy as a field. What we know and understand is shifting on multiple fronts constantly. Breakthroughs is to the series for works that push the boundaries—a place where all the books do more than contribute to the field, they remake the field in fundamental ways. Books are selected precisely because they change how we understand both education and the sociology of education.

Seeing with Poetic Eyes

Critical Race Theory and Moving from Liberal to Critical Forms of Race Research in Sociology of Education

Benjamin Blaisdell

SENSE PUBLISHERS
ROTTERDAM/BOSTON/TAIPEI

A C.I.P. record for this book is available from the Library of Congress.

ISBN 978-90-8790-772-3 (paperback)
ISBN 978-90-8790-773-0 (hardback)
ISBN 978-90-8790-774-7 (e-book)

Published by: Sense Publishers,
P.O. Box 21858, 3001 AW
Rotterdam, The Netherlands
http://www.sensepublishers.com

Printed on acid-free paper

Dedicated to my son, Pablo, for reminding me why this work is important and when it is time to play.

BREAKTHROUGHS IN THE SOCIOLOGY OF EDUCATION

This book series is seeking the unusual books in sociology of education. The usual books are working out the details of an already established paradigm of research and/or thought. These books are valuable for their contributions to confirming, elaborating, extending, fine tuning and critiquing aspects of established ways of thinking and studying. They are essential to getting things right within the paradigm they are working. The unusual books this series encourages do some of the above no doubt. Every study starts from somewhere. However, the unusual books are more about pushing boundaries, seeing things anew, and pursuing new paradigms of thought. I have titled the series *Breakthroughs* to signal this interest in the unusual books in the sociology of education.

Breakthroughs in any field are not easily categorized precisely because they tend to work away from the established but not necessarily in any patterned ways. While many book series have established themselves to pursue a particular promising line of thought, this is not my intention here. While I will encourage multiple books in any vein, I also wish to explore multiple veins. The goal is to encourage a wide range of approaches, each of which makes a claim to push the established boundaries of the sociology of education in some particular manner. The hope is that some of these new ideas and paradigms will be able to articulate what they offer over the established paradigms and if they prove sufficiently promising will become over time what we think of as usual ways of thinking in the sociology of education. Others may not become established as commonsense sociology but I intend with this series to celebrate both the spirit of experimentation and creativity that the sociology of education must have to progress.

It is in this spirit that I welcome Benjamin Blaisdell's book, *Seeing with Poetic Eyes,* as the first in the series. Critical race theory is relatively recent in its application in sociology of education but has captured the interest of many young scholars of race. It substantive theme is that race is central to the workings of American society and that property rights have trumped human and civil rights in these workings. Blaisdell reviews critical race theory for those who need an introduction but more importantly he is pushing the theory into application. Most critical race studies to date are limited to analysis and critique, but Dr. Blaisdell wanted to see how critical race theory plays with teachers who see themselves, in varying degrees, as allies of students of color. critiques the sociology of education and elaborates what critical race theory can offer the discipline. Sociology of education is after all a creation largely of whites and acts as a form of property itself. Dr. Blaisdell does much more than offer his critique as he works with teachers to examine their practice and what critical race theory offers it. *Seeing with Poetic Eyes* shows not only what the teachers learned from working with him in this but also how he learned as he worked from one teacher to the next. Here he shows how encounters at the level of practice can inform scholarship as well as how we are to work with those who will actually do the work of critical race theory with students.

I cannot think of a better book to begin this series, and I thank him for it. It pushes boundaries, challenges the extant paradigm of sociology of education, and reminds us that ideas are put to the ultimate test on the ground—not in theoretical works.

March 2009
George W. Noblit, *University of North Carolina at Chapel Hill*

TABLE OF CONTENTS

ACKNOWLEDGEMENTS

First, I want to thank all of the teachers in this study. I respect them for the work that they do, and I hope I continue to honor their commitment to education.

I want to thank the scholars who helped me complete this project. I thank Dwight Rogers and James Trier for being encouraging mentors and friends and for their on-going support. I thank Adrienne Davis for sharpening my understanding and analysis of critical race theory. I send a special thank you to Soyini Madison, who has welcomed me into the world of performance and taught me to "feel" the value it bestows. I send a very special thank you to George Noblit for beautifully balancing education with inspiration and for being able to guide me in the world of educational scholarship. George has provided me an incomparable level and quality of mentorship and has taught me to do this work with heart as well as mind.

I also thank my colleagues and friends for your feedback and welcome diversions. In particular, I thank Myriam Casimir being a sounding board during the writing process and Sherick Hughes for welcoming me as a scholar on race. Both Myriam and Sherick have helped me navigate the complexities involved in race work. I also thank Paula Grubbs for helping me find time to write.

Finally, I thank my parents for their unending support. I thank my mom, Carol, and my stepfather, Al, for their encouragement and faith in me. I thank my dad, Lincoln, for his constant enthusiasm and warmest care. I send a special thank you to my stepmother, Millie, for walking me through the tumult and joys of graduate school and of fatherhood and for literally being there for me in all of the crunch times.

CHAPTER 1

ADDRESSING LIBERALISM

Critical Race Theory as Dialogic Performance

In this book, I examine the ways in which white educators discuss and conceptualize race. I report on an ethnographic study in which I used critical race theory (CRT) in a dialogic performance with seven white teachers in order to open up conversations about how white teachers can support or resist colorblindness, white privilege, and white racial dominance. Based on this study, I explain how CRT can (1) help move white teachers from liberal to more critical understandings of racism and antiracism and (2) move the field of sociology of education to approaches to research on race that are also more critical in practice, thus following the more transformative aspects of the race work present in the field.

The conceptual framework I describe below focuses on how CRT can inform critical perspectives on race in sociology of education, specifically in how the field can uncover and work against liberal accounts of race. I point out how in the field of sociology of education, scholarship already exists that uncovers white racism. I also point out that scholarship in the field already exists that exposes liberal ideology, an ideology that often supports institutional forms of racism. At the same time, as a teacher educator who has attempted to use the scholarship in the field to challenge white racism and much of its liberal underpinnings, I have had a hard time using much of the empirical research in the field to pursue the more transformative agenda/intentions of critical research. CRT offered me a useful way to pursue such an agenda.

Liberalism persists in schools (Apple, 2004) and in the thinking and practice of white teachers (e.g., see Kailin, 1999) and this persistence can negatively affect students of colors other than white. Sociology of education can challenge this liberalism (and has to some extent), but to more effectively work against those negative effects, I believe the field needs to further its development of critical approaches to what Morrow (2000) calls "mediational" analyses, especially when examining the persistence of liberalism and institutional racism in schools. So, in this book, I discuss how sociology of education can take advantage of the critical theory strain in the field and use CRT to combat liberal interpretations of race when conducting research on race.

In the study I employed a performance approach to research, which was useful in examining and even challenging the liberalism of the teachers in the study. The performance approach encouraged me to focus on the pedagogical aspects of the research (Denzin, 2003) not only in the traditional sense of how the data informs the field but also in the more reflective sense of how the research act itself informed my participants as potentially antiracist teachers and me as a potentially antiracist researcher and teacher educator. In this sense, performance methodology—and dialogic performance, in particular, which I discuss later in this chapter—enabled me to develop and pursue a more critical methodology.

As one of my goals with the book is to comment on sociology of education, I briefly discuss how the field traditionally has examined race. I focus the following conceptual framework on how empirical—and primarily qualitative—studies in the field are not always as effective at challenging liberal interpretations of race as they could be. I, then, use the framework to set up an argument about how CRT can foster more critical interpretations and, thus, promote more critical research practices. I do not intend to argue that no empirical studies that pursue a critical line of inquiry exist but rather that it is often the case that these studies offer only limited ways to use their research to challenge racism in whites that do not already adhere to more critical understandings of race.

As Morrow (2000) argues, "the dominant tendency in critical pedagogy is—despite much rhetoric to the contrary—to presume normative stances without pursuing the more complex strategy of dialogical communicative ethics…" (59–60). Basically, Morrow claims that much of the qualitative work in critical sociology of education does not discuss how to effectively analyze both the structural and agential dimensions of institutional oppression. He argues that much of the qualitative research that adheres to a critical theory perspective fails to "deal conceptually and analytically with…concrete power relations and structures of domination" (60).[1] My claim is similar to Morrow's. Specifically, while I believe critical theory has been effective in critiquing liberalism,[2] empirical studies on race in the field of sociology of education have often fallen short in developing a critical ethnographic methodology that can be used to counter that liberalism.

As Gallagher (2000) argues, studies—including his own—that uncover racist comments from white participants fail to challenge the participants on the underlying logic of such comments. Rather, the "objective interviewer stance" of such studies "absolves the researcher and informant of the responsibility of challenging white racism and white privilege" (72–73). Most of the studies do not take on the goal of challenging racism as part of the direct research act, so they do not attempt to develop effective analytical techniques with which to work against structures of racial domination in school settings. Even the qualitative studies rely on what Denzin (2003) calls ethnographic textualism. Ethnographic textualism views data collection as a means to ascertain some sort of material truth about a given context rather than as a means of creating an interpretation of events or conditions in that setting. When studies rely on what is essentially a post-positivist understanding of data, they fail to position the research act as a transformative event. That is not to say that these studies do not offer valuable insight. However, a reliance on ethnographic textualism prevents the researchers from making the transformative possibilities of their research explicit, a step that could make these studies better achieve the transformative goals of critical theory itself. Furthermore, relying on ethnographic textualism prevents researchers from working against their complicity in "validat[ing] and justify[ing] the existing racial hierarchy that privileges whites" (Gallagher, 72). My goal in this book, then, is to discuss how CRT can be used in a more dialogic approach to research on race, an approach that like many before it uncovers white racism but that also does not absolve itself of challenging white racism.

I discuss the potential transformative possibilities of a dialogic approach in the context of education research by specifically discussing how CRT can be used with whites (and white teachers specifically) towards developing dispositions and practices that counter liberal interpretations of race and racism. Such an approach can inform research in the sociology of education that has an agenda of combating racism can make its goals and possibilities for transformation more explicit

CONCEPTUAL FRAMEWORK

I want to put forth a couple of caveats before I discuss my claims about the field of sociology of education. First of all, while I critique the field of sociology of education and its employment of critical theory, I also want to be clear that both have enabled the development of more critical and comprehensive studies of race in education. Second of all, my critiques stem from my own experiences as a researcher and teacher educator who focuses on issues of race and racism. The limitations I have found in the field are based in my ability (and inability) to use empirical studies in the field to understand and communicate the existence and nature of institutional racism in education. My critique is not intended as an all-emncompassing denunciation of sociology of education but rather more as a formative assessment from my standpoint as a budding resarcher and educator in the field. In this conceptual framework, I explain the way in which the remnants of liberalism in the field, in addition to in educational settings, hinder the political and transformative project of critical theory. The backdrop for this explication is my experience as a teacher educator and researcher who has attempted to use sociology of education to develop a dialogic method of the critical examination of institutional racism. It has been my experience that liberalism is one of the key impediments to moving white teachers to more critical understandings of race. My intent is neither to overstate the existence or influence of liberalism in the field nor to understate the ability of the field to develop more critical transformative projects. Rather, my goal is to propose one direction the field can take to challenge liberalism in educational settings, overcome the liberal remnants in empirical sociological research, and further the field's potential in developing such critical projects.

Sociology of Education

Sociology of education has long been concerned with examining race and racism and in working against racial inequity in schools. The broader field of sociology has provided a firm basis from which to study race.

> Sociologists of race deeply contextualize race and racism by historicizing race within the context of unequal social relations. Next, they help to shed light on the inextricable links between race and class and explore how race can be manipulated and constructed to benefit certain groups and disadvantage

> others. Like critical race theorists in the law, sociologists of race call for a deeper understanding of racism that locates it at the very center of social, political and economic relations in society. (Lynn and Parker, 2006)

Recent work in sociology of education has analyzed, in particular, the existence of institutional racism (e.g., McNamee & Miller, 2004; Ballantine, 2001; Oakes, Wells, Jones, and Datnow, 1997; Fischer, Hout, Jaankowski, Lucas, Swidler and Voss, 1996; Omi and Winant, 1994). Furthermore, very recent studies (Feagin and O'Brien, 2003; Myers, 2003) have furthered seminal work of scholars like Frankenburg (1993) and examined the perpetuation of institutional racism via the everyday actions of individual actors. In this section, I examine and critique how the field of sociology of education addresses issues of race and racism with regard to liberal ideology—highlighting the field's strengths, limitations, and possibilities—in order to then examine in the following section how CRT can further the field. In particular, I will argue how CRT can help sociology of education analyze and work against the presence of liberalism in teacher thinking as well as provide mechanisms for empirical research in the field to more closely connect the research act with a challenge to instances of institutional racism, potentially overcoming the remnants of liberalism that remain in the field itself.

The Influence of Critical Theory

Freeman (1990) explains why it is hard for people with racial privilege—and specifically whites—to envision broader structural change when he describes the concept of perpetrator versus victim perspectives. In his early piece of CRT, he explains how racialized groups of people that have not been traditionally marginalized hold on to a perpetrator perspective of the world. In this view, people believe they are free from complicity in racism, except for those few who actually perpetrate overt acts of racism. Therefore, remedies to racism exist only in controls on those few individuals. Alternatively, those who come from racialized groups that have been traditionally marginalized hold onto a victim perspective of the world. In this view, racism is a condition that permeates their lives more broadly. Since racism is a condition of life, the only way to end it is to address all the aspects of society that contribute to it. A victim perspective approach to the elimination of racism would require substantial changes in the structure of social institutions like education. Liberal ideology promotes a perpetrator view of racism. In the field of law, for example, the dominance of liberal ideology is apparent in policy and legal decisions that fall short of radical structural changes and that view institutional decisions that privilege racial minorities as unfair to whites, who allegedly have no direct role in overt racism.[3]

In contrast to liberalism then, critical theory takes structural aspects of racism into account, attempts to work from a victim perspective of racism, and critiques social institutions more substantially. Issues such racism and sexism are not mere fissures in the structure of society but rather inherent to structure of social institutions themselves. Therefore, the goal of critical theory is to change those structures more radically. Part of why critical theory can envision more radical change than liberalism does is because of how race is conceptualized in critical theory. Liberal accounts of race tend to hold onto hold onto static, even biological, notions of race. This type of vision of race fails to examine the historical and social construction of racial categorization. Gotanda (1995) argues that these accounts of race fail to examine the political construction of race, i.e. race becomes an apolitical categorization (p. 259). This type of categorization can lead to oversimplified remedies to racism, such as an over-reliance on integration in lieu of other possibilities. The argument is that if these racial groups (black, white, Latino, etc.), which are defined as fixed categories, are integrated into society—i.e., that they legally have the same rights as privileges as whites—then their lives will be better and society in general will be better off. Critical theory problematizes this view by analyzing how the construction of these categories has contributed to and continues to contribute to subjugation, even if integration and equal rights appear to exist. In its view that racial categories are socially and politically constructed, critical theory can historicize those constructions and analyze who gains and who loses in apparent attempts at racial remedy.

Critical theory's understanding of the historical/political construction of race influences the way in which theory is used. Drawing from the developments of Marxist thought and the Frankfurt School, critical theory uses theory as a transformative activity. Since truth is contextual and political, theory is not important as a way to find absolute truth but rather as a mechanism to effect social change. Theory becomes about contextual action and not truth-seeking.[4] The implications for this approach on how to address inequality in education are significant. Giroux (2001) argues that where liberal accounts of education don't challenge the institution of schooling—i.e., they look at its continuity—critical theory looks for the breaks in that continuity. Rather than try to uncover instances of racism within institutions such as schools, critical theory attempts to uncover what he refers to as the hidden curriculum of schools, which itself may be racist. For example, critical theory would look at how tracking segregates students, illuminating how it claims to give students what they need (according to a social efficiency view of curriculum) but actually discriminates against students along racial and class lines. Giroux points out that critical theory has been influential in the way in which sociology of education analyzes issues such as racism.

The Persistence of Liberalism

At the same time, however, as Giroux (1997) also points out, liberalism in educational discourse persists in ways that continue to frame students as needy or deprived (of culture, experiences, etc.). In analyzing social injustice, liberalism focuses on individuals rather than on social groups or the structure of societal institutions in conceptualizing social change (Apple, 2004; Popkewitz, 1998). That is to say, a liberal approach to challenging racism would look at individuals who were overtly racist and might enact laws that prevent these types of racist acts on other individuals. In following this individualistic approach to resolving injustice, a liberal interpretation of the institution of education promotes principles that resist a more critical understanding of how the institution produces racial disparity. First, liberalism values neutrality. In education, this means that teachers believe schools to be culturally neutral in structure. Thus, the school rules, in-class discourse, and curriculum are assumed not to promote any one culture over another. In such a viewpoint there is no acknowledgement then of the link of those structures to whiteness. Second, therefore, liberalism promotes colorblindness. As institutions are culturally neutral, acknowledging racial difference and making decisions based on race are themselves practices betray fairness. Schools are assumed to be culturally neutral, so they do not privilege one race over another. As racial privilege does not exist for any group including whites, to make a decision based on race would thus be unfair and would not support a liberal approach equity.

Such a colorblind view of equity only recognizes intentional forms of racism. Since the institution itself is fair towards all, it cannot possibly marginalize any group of students based on race or any other cultural difference. Instances of racism are anomalies (not systemically inherent) and racial disparity is not caused by the institution itself. Rather, such disparity must stem from either these anomalies (which are intentional acts by those who do not follow the institution's rules) or from outside sources (and in educational settings, teachers might name these sources as economics/poverty or the culturally deficient home lives of people from certain cultures). Therefore, the solutions to racial disparity do not exist at the institutional level. Instead, racial equity can be achieved by working against those anomalies or by addressing those factors that do not fall under the responsibility of the social institution. This might include working against those who practice explicit, intentional forms of racism. It might also include claiming that the responsibility for racial equity lays outside of the school or even with those who actually suffer the consequences of disparity. If only they had better resources or their families valued education more, racial equity could be achieved.

For example, in the case of school desegregation, laws were created to make it illegal to deny an individual access to a school or a class strictly because a student is a member of a racial minority. Such laws do not contradict a liberal ideological approach to social change, where the focus of change is on individuals or policies that overtly discriminate against racial minorities. In addition, such laws do not require those who are complicit in institutional racism to change their ideology with regards to the causes of racial disparity. That ideology dictates the normalized practices within schools and classroom—e.g., tracking or disciplinary practices—that disproportionately affect students of color. Since there is no dramatic change in how schools are run day-to-day, those practices can continue to affect students of color. In fact, with the official and overt barriers to equal resources out of the way, the victims of racism have the responsibility to also change their behavior if they are to access "equal" opportunities, resources, etc. In this way, liberalism promotes a slow, incremental approach to social change. Laws change first, which will eventually lead to a more egalitarian society as those who have been the victims of racism adapt to the existing structure of society and its institutions. This law-by-law approach does not radically challenge social institutions (rather it works through them), does not historicize those institutions, and does not examine or utilize the relationship between ideological and material change, in effect not sufficiently affecting either.

Omi and Winant (1994) provide a concise explanation of how liberalism fails to challenge institutional racism. They claim that liberalism fails to acknowledge the inherent racism of the state and its policies.

> The argument is that state actions in the past and present have treated people in very different ways according to their race, and thus the government cannot retreat from its policy responsibilities in this area. It [the state] cannot suddenly declare itself "color-blind" without in fact perpetuating the same type of differential, racist treatment. (57)

Liberal interpretations of race, which do in fact make such colorblind claims without historicizing societal institutions such as education, do not link race to social structure. Government initiatives that simply create new policies that attempt to counter racism without partaking in a broader antiracist agenda that includes a critique and analysis of the government and its history of racism will in fact perpetuate racism. Therefore, institutions like the government need to develop approaches to antiracism in a more comprehensive way. To use Omi and Winant's phrase, the government (like other social institutions) needs to "fulfill its responsibility to uphold a robust conception of equality" (58), particularly with regards to race. Liberalism, by claiming the government and its policies to be colorblind, fails to rearticulate race in such a broad way. It does not critique the inherent and historical existence of institutional racism and relies on individual policies to counter racism.

Furthermore, liberalism fails to effectively counter institutional racism because it does not connect its definition of race to social structure. Omi and Winant (1994) explain that racial formation is "the sociohistorical process by which racial categories are created, inhabited, transformed, and destroyed" (p. 55) and that such formation is racist if it "creates or reproduces structures of domination based on essentialist categories of race" (p. 71). So, when race is defined only in relation to "interest group, class fraction, nationality, or cultural identity" (p. 111), the connection to the social and political agendas that control the construction of racial categories and hierarchies is missed. Specific racial interest groups or cultural identities, for example, have been developed in response to that socio-political construction of race. The liberal view does not acknowledge the socio-political forces that continue to influence the development of those group affiliations and racial identities. Rather, it sees them more statically. By failing to link its conception of race to how race is constructed by social and political structure(s), liberalism can only understand racism as something that was developed in the past and not as something that continues to be promoted. In contrast to critical theory, which attempts to focus on the on-going social construction of race, liberalism continues to envision the remedy for racial disparity, then, in individual policies, without recognizing how those policies allow institutional racism to be perpetuated. As Apple (2004) and Dale (1976) have argued, the institution, along with its policies and standardized practices, becomes the remedy for social inequities like racial disparity.

Liberalism in Empirical Studies of Race in Sociology

This type of liberal interpetation of race still exists in some empirical studies in the sociology of education, particularly in discussions of the causes of racial disparity in schools and how that disdaprity can be overcome. Racial identity and group affiliation in such studies is more statically defined and the cultural practices that go with them are measured and categorized according to an un-named racial norm. The focus of such analyses is on individual or cultural factors that contribute to minority students' lack of academic achievement and not on the social and political structural practices that act on and marginalize those students. For example, *The Black-White Test Score Gap*, edited by Jencks and Phillips (1998), is a major work that tries to explain the gap in achievement on standardized tests between white and black students. While the study offers a comprehensive look at some of the factors that lead to the achievement gap, overall it fails to examine societal institutions such as schooling or the economic structure. The various authors, including Jencks and Phillips, do attempt to explain the persistence of the test score gap and at times try to shift blame away from the people who suffer most from it. For instance, they attack arguments that paint negative pictures of African American students' innate academic ability and they argue that schools should push more lower socioeconomic status (SES) students into honors and advanced placement (AP) courses. However, the language they use and the paradigm of thought they employ do not include an analysis of how social institutions contribute to the conditions that minority and lower SES students live in. For example, they discuss how parenting practices have "more impact on children's cognitive development than preschool practices" (p. 46) and how changing these practices (in addition to school changes) can positively affect this development. However, they never discuss the disconnect between school culture and home culture. They do not discuss the sociopolitical factors that affect those parental practices. While their intent is a broad look at both the causes of and solutions to the test score gap, their analysis and discussion is acontextual. More importantly, it is apolitical. For example, they call for theories that "pay more attention to the way family members and friends interact with each other" (p. 43), but they do not discuss how one type of interaction may be more valued in educational settings than another or how the racial nature of these interactions may affect how that valuation. In this way, their focus is on uncovering information that could lead to changes in educational practice and policy. They do not discuss how educational practice and policy themselves lead to the achievement gap. In this way they fail to incorporate a social structural interpretation of race and racism.

There are other examples of sociology of education that take similar approaches to the study of race (e.g., Hallinan, 1994; Kao, Tienda, & Schneider, 1996; Kalmijn & Kraaykamp, 1996). While these studies may highlight where inequality exists in school and examine the differences in the characteristics of various racial groups, most unintentionally put the blame for unequal academic achievement on individuals and on their families, cultural practices and communities, failing to acknowledge institutional factors that act on students' lives. Similar to the studies in Jencks and Phillip's volume, these works either do not take a strong social structural look at schooling or limit their structural analysis to individual policies. For the most part, in accordance with liberal ideology, they limit their interpretations of the existence of racism in institutions as fissures that can be mended by changes in behavior by the victims of racism. Furthermore, the mending process they envision is one that does not overtly call for any more drastic change in the current structure of schooling.

Studies That Challenge Liberalism. Sociologists of education have also attempted to work against that type of liberal discourse. Though I will point out some of the limitations of these scholars, what is common to all is their desire to work against the dominant discourses in education, which Giroux (1997) argues, "fail to understand how schools are implicated in reproducing oppressive ideologies and social practices" (p. 130). The strengths of the works I cite in the next three sections is that they do account for schools' complicity in the reproduction of institutional racism and they do offer useful analyses that help uncover that complicity. My critique of the studies in the following two sections focuses on their lack of developing a way to counter such complicity. They do not extensively develop any mediational analyses.[5] I understand that such an analytical approach was not the intent of these studies, but I critique them in order to argue that more work on race in the field is needed, particularly work that follows the motivation of critical theory and makes explicit the processes that can effectively counter institutional racism. Furthermore, by not challenging (or even discussing how to challenge) the white racism that is uncovered, these studies may actually promote inferential racism (Gallagher, 2000, drawing from Hall [1981]). In essence, by using the research act to get whites to express racist views and then not challenging the problematic premises of these views, researchers may actually allow such racist viewpoints to perpetuate themselves.

Studies That Examine Structural Practices. A good example of sociological research that does focus on uncovering the way in which educational institutional practices and policies do contribute to racial disparity is the work of Oakes, et al. (1997) in their analysis of school tracking practices. These authors show how attempts to detrack can actually be seen as threats to the institution of schooling. Although they acknowledge that detracking does not automatically guarantee students of color a better education, their analysis does highlight the detrimental effects of tracking and illuminates the politics of decisions to track or detrack. Thus, their work begins to look more closely at the political nature of how schools are structured in ways that contribute to racism.

The above example also shows that the perpetrator perspective is still prevalent in schooling, even in attempts at racial remedy. When schools detrack, parents with privilege can still manipulate school sites to maintain that privilege for their children. Therefore, as the analysis by Oakes, et al. (1997) shows, simple decisions that change one aspect of an educational institution can make it appear that racism has been addressed without actually affecting the institution's inherent deeper racist roots, roots that cause the structure itself to be racist. Scholars such as Oakes who employ a critical theory approach attempt to take a victim perspective on inequality, highlighting how singular changes such as detracking may not affect the deeper structure that maintains white privilege and racism with the hope of opening up space for more radical school change. A critique I have, as mentioned earlier, is that even though this research interprets the nature of racism in more critical and structural ways, it also often fails to address the material ways that change can be promoted. Furthermore, because the research adheres to traditional research roles, it fails to offer examples of how to use the research act itself for more immediate transformative ends. While I agree with Morrow (2000) that not all critical research needs to be participatory action research, I also believe that sociologists who follow critical perspectives need to develop research approaches that highlight potential ways to counter institutionally marginalizing practices, especially if they do not want to promote the inferential racism that Gallagher (2000) and Hall (1981) warn against. In the end, adherence to only traditional research approaches can limit researchers' ability to achieve the transformative agenda of their work.

Studies That Examine Teacher Thought And Discourse. Another way recent work in sociology has critically analyzed race has been via studies that examine how people think about and discuss race. In these studies, sociology of education has been very useful in uncovering how race continues to be constructed in ways that lead to institutional racism (e.g., Frankenburg, 1993; Hytten and Warren, 2003). More recently, this work has been specifically effective in uncovering the links between white privilege and racism. For example, there have been recent studies that analyze how whites talk about race and how such talk is connected to various forms of racism (e.g.; Feagin and O'Brien; 2003, Myers; 2005). Feagin and O'Brien (2005) investigate how whites in positions with a certain amount of power either adhere to or work against racist attitudes and practices. Their rationale is that these whites have a certain amount of influence on the "social strata" and "social networks" (p. 28) which make up our society and thus uncovering their racial understandings is important to eventually work against racism. Myers (2003) similarly hopes to uncover how people, and not just whites, talk about race, especially in negative ways, which she calls racetalk. Her goals are to highlight such racetalk so as to show how it still exists in society and to comment on the damage that such talk can do, and she claims/implies that this illumination will help people challenge the practice of racetalk.

While my study is similar to these in that it also is a study of whites talking about race, there are some key differences as well. Perhaps the most significant difference is in the research approach itself. As I stated above, these studies have been very effective and useful in describing how racism is connected to white privilege and how the on-going construction of race contributes to that privilege. They follow Omi and Winant's (1994) claim that understandings of race and racism have to be connected to social structures. However, similar to studies that examine structural practices such as Oakes (1997), these studies do not link their analyses to practices that can counter the racism they analyze. Put another way, because they, too, stick to traditional research roles they do not pursue an extensively mediational analysis of racism and do not directly challenge the white racism they uncover.

Studies That Model Critical Methodology. Some studies in the field do break away from these traditional research roles and pursue a mediational agenda. A key example is *Subtractive Schooling* by Angela Valenzuela (1997). While Valenzuela is not explicit about developing a methodology to counter the institutional oppression she encounters, she does pursue a more critical research approach in her use of both methodology and theory. In her research, she did this in part by attempting to use the privilege and position as researchers to affect material change in the school she studied. For example, she involved herself immediately (to paraphrase Denzin [2003]) and worked to mediate a confrontation between a teacher and his students. Furthermore, Valenzuela's analysis consciously narrates the actions of the students (actions that can be interpreted as resistant to school policies and practices) and of the teacher (a culturally responsive and caring teacher) in critically racially conscious ways. She puts the both the students' and the teacher's behavior in the context of the social structure of the school. Thus, her analysis resists a liberal interpretation of the students' and teacher's actions that would ignore how those actions were influences by the policies and practices of the school itself. In doing so, Valenzuela takes a critical ethnography approach to research, an approach that uses the research act to challenge "taken-for-granted assumptions by bringing to light underlying and obscure operations of power and control" (Madison, 2005, p. 5). Furthermore, she inserts herself in the research setting in way in which she can affect change immediately.[6] In fact, such an approach—one that both puts students actions in the context of larger institutional structures and that involves the research as an active participant in is more common in Latino education and LatCrit.[7]

In her study of white, female pre-service teachers, McIntyre (1997) had a similar agenda, and in fact, her approach is perhaps the most similar to mine. She employed what she calls a participatory action research approach to heighten the critical consciousness (regarding race) of the participants in her study. While her agenda may have been explicit as mine if attempting to change the views of her research participants,[8] she did attempt to challenge some of their views on race and whiteness, especially as those views diverted the issues away from the responsibilities of whites and at times justified certain types of racetalk (or what McIntyre calls white talk). My study attempts a similar approach to McIntyre's and incorporates into it a more explicit dialogic analysis of race via the use of CRT. Perhaps some differences between our projects (which in no way diminish the power of McIntyre's project) are that I take this type of study to in-service teachers (who have more school-specific experiences to draw on in our dialogue) and that I do not focus in any depth on the construction white identity (which is certainly a strength of McIntyre's study). By discussing with teachers their perspectives of daily classroom life, my focus is on how white teachers support or resist institutional forms of racism.

Reconsidering the Sociology of Education

I want to reiterate that I believe the field has long been concerned with fore-fronting the relationship between race and educational inequity. New scholarship exists (such as the examples above) that recognizes the importance of centering race in its analysis. The intent of my critique has been to point out that persistence of liberalism in much of the empirical research and how that liberalism can mitigate the transformative potential of research that has an antiracist agenda. While many of the researchers I cited do acknowledge the on-going social structural construction of race, the liberal remnants that remain exist in how the studies promote a challenge to racism. All but a very few studies, even those that employ the most critical interpretations of racism, fail to discuss how to uncover racism in their participants and also how to then challenge that racism more immediately in the research act. McIntyre (1997) and Frankenburg (1993) both discuss how raising awareness about white racism does not necessarily lead to participants changing what they do (and my study falls into that same trap). McIntyre even raises concerns similar to those articulated by Gallagher (2000) that allowing the white participants to discuss their views of race actually allowed them to maintain racist views. Because of the research approaches they employ, their intent is not to challenge racism in such an immediate sense. However, by not making a link to potential antiracist practices, the studies assume that their analyses—which are indeed important and informative—will lead to some progress towards the elimination of racism. This assumption itself falls into the trap of liberal ideology in that it assumes that the structures in place in academia will lead to transformation in institutional thought and practice. I am not asserting that scholarship should *only* lead clearly to direct action. I reiterate my agreement with Morrow (2000) that participatory action research is not the only form of research that can fall under the label of critical theory research. However, to avoid perpetuating inferential racism, I do believe that as researchers of race in particular, we should not be satisfied with following traditional research roles (especially if we adhere to many of the tenets of critical theory) and traditional avenues for recommending and affecting change. Therefore, my claim in this book, then, is that sociologists of education need to be more determinant and explicit in making the link between their analyses and potentially antiracist practices. In that sense, this book is a call to scholars of race—especially white scholars of race—to make our work more immediate in our agenda of antiracism. The hope is that research in the field can continue to move in more critically antiracist directions.

Toward that end, my study has an objective that is similar to Feagin and O'Brien's (2003) and to Myers' (2005) in that I want to highlight certain discourse with the hope that such exposure will help educators challenge it. However, drawing on the motivation of CRT to challenge racism (and not just study it) and on Ladson-Billings' (1998) call to make this work relevant to teachers and students, I have attempted to use CRT to directly affect the practice of teachers in the study. Rather than only examine the phenomena of racetalk and extract information from my co-performers, I attempted to also challenge the colorblind and liberal views contained in such talk. I do not at all mean to indicate that studies like Feagin and O'Brien's and Myers' are less useful than mine. On the contrary, they are fuller articulations of the complicated dynamics of racetalk. The scope of their studies exceeded mine in their examination of how whites talk about race and are especially useful in uncovering the key underlying ideologies that whites employ. The strength of my study is that I start to examine how to challenge racetalk and the colorblind ideology that supports it. My attempt has been to enact a mediational analysis that links critical social theory with a qualitative methodological approach that examines and challenges institutional racism. CRT was key for me in making this link.

Critical Race Theory

CRT is very much in line with critical theory in several ways. In CRT, theory is certainly a transformational, political act. It moves away from empiricism and positivism, especially as traditionally defined. It also retains a structural critique of social institutions. Critical race scholars would agree with Giroux (2001) that this critique must include the voices of traditionally silenced groups. CRT, however, would not see the need, as Giroux does, to highlight the importance of the Frankfurt school. Because it comes from the Frankfurt school, this version of critical theory comes from a European tradition that might not adequately represent or speak to the experiences of non-whites. Structural critique, then, must come from the margins, from new perspectives.[9] Matsuda (1995/1987) describes the need to look to the bottom. Those who have experienced injustices such as racism, in fact those who are the continual victims of it, have a better understanding of that perspective. Just as civil rights lawyers often pursued their own agenda (rather than that of the parents they claimed to be fighting for) in school desegregation cases (Bell, 1995/1976), scholars who are not victims of racism may not be the most appropriate to lead the fight against racism. This is not to say that white scholars cannot do work against racism but that they should let scholars of color take the lead in the pursuit of this agenda (Delgado, 1995/1984; Guinier & Torres, 2002).

Equally important in CRT is that while sociologists of education often parallel race and class, CRT centers race. This is not to say that CRT scholars think class (or gender or language background for that matter) is unimportant. Rather, they believe that race has played a significant and central role in discrimination in society and social institutions like schools (Ladson-Billings, 1998). In fact, by centering race, CRT scholars believe that these other social ills can be addressed as well and that all forms of injustice can be examined for their intersectionality (Guinier & Torres, 2002; Delgado & Stefancic, 2001). One of the primary ways that CRT centers race is by analyzing how racism is created and maintained via a system of norms rooted in whiteness. "Once we understand how our categories, tools, and doctrines influence us, we may escape their sway and work more effectively for liberation" (Delgado and Stefancic, 2000, p. 213). For whites, this understanding must include an awareness of how those categories, tools, and doctrines make us complicit in racism. The ways we set guidelines, organize knowledge, and create policy are rooted in and perpetuate white privilege, and

CRT can help us expose the creation of that privilege, a privilege that makes us complicit in racism.

In this way, CRT maintains a connection to whiteness studies, both which uncover and challenge practices of white privilege. At the same time, CRT and whiteness studies differ somewhat in how they challenge white privilege. Both highlight practices of whiteness that marginalize people of color. The difference is in the specific concepts that CRT offers (some of which will be described below) that can be used to analyze and challenge those practices. In addition, where whiteness studies is at least in part concerned with working towards positive white identity formation (Kincheloe and Steinberg, 1998; Rodriguez, 2000), CRT uses these concepts to work more exclusively at tearing down material and ideological barriers to racial equality, and in particularly institutional racism as sustained by the practice of white racial dominance.

This nexus of material and ideological change is important for such social change to be sustained. The work of Iglesias (2002) and Delgado (1995/1984) shows that the ultimate goal of CRT is not to only change laws or rules but also to change ideology and action. Changing a rule within an institution without changing that institution's ideology will only allow the institution to maintain its current inequities (Iglesias, 2002). So, changing institutional ideologies is necessary. Changes in rules and law are part of this project but they are not the end goal and we cannot rely on rules and laws alone. Bell (1995/1976, 1995/1980) has shown how changing laws is not sufficient. Laws can be circumvented or accommodated to maintain privilege. Segregation still exists in schools, and in some regions segregation has increased recently (Laosa, 2001). As Oakes et al. (1997) have shown, schools maintain an in-school form of segregation via tracking. Furthermore, desegregation has not guaranteed equitable educational resources and opportunities for students of color (Bell, 1995/1976). So, changing (or at least engaging) institutional ideology is also necessary in order to bring about changes in institutional practices that can have positive effects on the lives of people of color. An example of this is the University of Texas decision to develop an admissions policy that involves racial and class awareness.[10] So, ideological change is a necessary to bring about material changes in people's lives, and in the end, material change is the goal of CRT. CRT doesn't fight for the idea of desegregation. It fights for better schools, better resources, and better curricula for people of color.[11]

Critical Race Theory and Naming Whiteness

One of the primary ways CRT accomplishes this socio-political agenda is via an analysis of white racial dominance, or what I call naming whiteness.[12] Following certain primary tenets, CRT analysis can explain the existence of white ways of seeing and being in very concrete ways, and it is this concreteness that makes it so useful as a critically transformative research approach. I have discussed these tenets along with CRT's analysis of whiteness in other work (Blaisdell, 2005a, 2005b). Below, I summarize that work as I describe what I mean by naming whiteness.

Naming whiteness involves uncovering concrete and specific examples of how white privilege is maintained by institutional practices, and it includes an analysis of how those practices are maintained in both material and ideological ways. That is to say, institutional practices that perpetuate white privilege and dominance are the result of the specific practices of individuals and the relationship of those privileges to dominant ideologies. As I quoted from Delgado and Stefancic (2000) above, those practices and the ideologies from which they stem create and reify ways of categorization that afford or deny privilege. Therefore, the goal is to name those practices for the way in which they perpetuate racial dominance and to connect them to their adherence to and support of such ideologies. By focusing on how individuals are a legitimating and reproducing component of the construction of institutional racism, naming whiteness does not ignore that institutional racism has actors (i.e., it isn't merely a monolithic "system" that exists beyond the scope of redress) and it allows for a conceptualization of agency (i.e., an ability to develop practices that do not merely support the dominant ideologies) that can occur in relation to the structure(s) contextualizing people's lives. In other words, naming whiteness is a way to construct a mediational analysis that concurrently addresses (1) both social structure and individual agency and (2) both material and ideological change.

The first tenet that supports CRT's analysis of whiteness is that racism is inherent to the structure of the societal institutions of the U.S. (Delgado & Stefancic, 2000). Therefore, it counters the liberal understanding of racism as a set of abnormal occurrences that can be eliminated one-by-one. As the inherent-ness of racism is perpetuated by an ideology that fails to acknowledge its existence, what becomes important for CRT is to critique colorblindness. In school settings, this involves uncovering how school policies and norms privilege whites over non-whites. Scholars have illustrated how those policies and norms are rooted in whiteness and how they negatively affect students of color (Ladson-Billings, 1998; Apple, 2000). So, a goal in using CRT with educators, and with white educators in particular, is to expose the normalcy of racism and perpetuate an understanding that we enact white ways of seeing and being (Blaisdell, 2005a) that help sustain white racial dominance.

Another key tenet that can help researchers communicate white's complicity and name whiteness is the concept of whiteness as property. As Harris (1995/1993) explains, whiteness exists as a form of property that helps whites use and enjoy certain privileges, exclude those deemed not to be white from those privileges, and debase that which does not correspond to a white cultural standard. Researchers of race in education can explain how this process exists in the regulations of schools and the dispositions and actions of school personnel. In other words, researchers can uncover the ways in which educators categorize their students based on the white norms those students are able to live up to. As the ownership of whiteness confers benefits to those who have it and denies them to those that do not, the connection can then be made to how educators dole out or hold back curricular and instructional resources based on how their students adhere to and succeed based on white norms. Thus, the link can be made to how this whiteness as a form of property controls the equitable access to educational resources and success. In making this link, researchers can again point out the specific practices of individual educators in their specific school contexts so as to make the connection between micro and macro level process—i.e., between individual practice and institutional, societal structures.

When the educational practices of whites are then named for their whiteness—i.e., when white ways of seeing and being are exposed for how they execute whiteness as a form of property—researchers can then work to "revision" (Delgado and Stefancic, 2000) the existence of institutional racism. That is to say, researchers can help explain institutional racism as a phenomena that exists because of how whites privilege whiteness through their actions and because of how they adhere to ideologies—such as liberalism—that mask how those actions make them complicit in white racial dominance. Traditionally, CRT has used narrative or counterstory (Delgado & Stefancic, 2001; Solórzano & Delgado Bernal, 2001) to offer new accounts of racism that unmask its normality and that include the complicity of whites. As history is a tool that has been used by whites to maintain privilege, traditional accounts of history have left out the voices of the marginalized. Therefore, CRT uses narratives from these groups (in essence, looking to the bottom) to challenge the assumed neutrality and race-less-ness of those accounts, thus historicizing institutions and highlighting the voices of people of color. Researchers of race in education can similarly use the analysis of whiteness to create critical accounts of racism in school settings.

CRT's implications for sociology of education lie in its ability to extend a critical examination of race to a critical methodology of race. In particular, I find that CRT's specific analysis of whiteness lends itself well to a mediational approach to research. This analysis is similar to the recent work in the field that links how race is practiced in daily life to the institutional structures that treat people who have been categorized as non-white differently to those who have been categorized as white. In that way, CRT maintains the connection of materiality to ideology and of the individual to the structural in its analysis. In fact, naming whiteness furthers the project of sociologists like Myers (2005) and Feagin and O'Brien (2003) because it offers an approach that breaks the dichotomy between macro-level and micro-level analysis in the development of critically antiracist research. CRT can further such research by making researchers consider the political nature of how they represent and interpret their findings and by paying close attention to how they respond to white racism as occurs in a more immediate sense in the research process.

PERFORMANCE ETHNOGRAPHY AND THE CHALLENGE TO LIBERALISM

I began this study by using CRT to examine the concept of colorblindness through the eyes of teachers in order to understand how teachers' beliefs in colorblindness relate to their teaching practices. In my conversations with teachers, I moved from an examination of colorblindness, to one of whiteness, and then to discussions of race and racism more broadly. The hope was to dialogue with teachers about race in order to affect perceptions and practices that privilege whiteness and marginalize students of color. The teachers in this study all wanted to work towards racial equity. They all already adhered to some practices that promoted that equity. In addition, none of them adhered to extreme forms of liberalism in their antiracist practices. Therefore, my intent with them became uncovering and eventually working against the remnants of liberalism in their approaches to racial equity. In effect, what I attempted to do in this study was to challenge the liberal aspects of the the teachers' personal ideologies and professional practices with the hope that they could use the social justice motivations they already possessed to develop more critical forms of antiracism. Using CRT helped me develop a conceptual framework for this goal. In essence, CRT aided me in an attempt to move the teachers towards more critical approaches to antiracism so that they could better realize the goals of equity they already carried with them. A performance ethnography approach to research, and in particular the practice of dialogic performance, was key in this attempt.

According to Denzin (2003) and Conquergood (1985, 1998), a performance approach challenges the maintaining of analytic distance from the participants, as this type of distance cannot lead to new ways of coming to understand the world. Rather, "[p]erformance approaches to knowing insist on immediacy and involvement" (Denzin, 2003, p. 8). The implication for such an approach in my study was that I had to focus on the research with teachers as an act where we came to understand the world in new ways, as an act of meaning making, and as an act that had relevance to the teachers themselves. Denzin asserts that performative research acts are inherently political—i.e., they are investigative processes that look at and critique events, the context in which those events occur, and even the people involved. In this study, the interviews with teachers became performances where the teachers and I examined and critiqued teachers' experiences with race, racism, colorblindness, and whiteness.

In performance ethnography, the research act itself is a performance. The primary purpose of the research act is not intended for the researcher to extract knowledge from the participants. Rather, researcher and participants take the role of co-performers (Conquergood, 1991) in meaning making. From this standpoint, I look at the interview process as a reflexive act of what Langellier and Peterson (2004) refer to as storytelling and performing narrative.

> Storytelling is performative in that the possibilities for our participation are marked out in advance, so to speak, by the discourse and by our material conditions. Stories also live after as well as live before performance. When we participate in storytelling…we reenact storytelling as a conventionalized form of communication as well as collaborate in the production of a unique story or performance. This story-telling event recites, recalls, reiterates previous storytelling events in general and in particular. In brief, storytelling is socially and culturally reflexive...because it is reflexive, any particular storytelling event has the potential to disrupt material constraints and discourse conventions and give rise to new possibilities for other storytelling events and for how we participate in performing narrative. (p. 4)

The discourse that the teachers and I performed on race, then, drew on our previous racial understandings and the racial stories we had heard and told in the past. At the same time, by being dialogic, the joint storytelling in which we participated in during this research helped us tell racial stories in new ways, potentially helping us come to new understandings.

In this reflexive sense, storytelling "can work both to legitimate and to critique relations of power" (Langellier and Peterson, 2004, p. 25). By using CRT to analyze the teachers' conversations, discourses, and classroom practices, I did maintain the role of expert research/ethnographer who could determine the meaning of what the research participants did and said, but using a performance approach tempered this role. "The language of drama and performance [gives…] a way of thinking and talking about people as actors who creatively play, interpret, improvise, interpret, and re-present roles and scripts" (Conquergood, 1991, p. 187). In this study, the performance was an act of meaning making around race, whiteness, and colorblindness. This was an act that the participants and I performed together, and it was my hope that we did this in ways that critiqued rather than legitimated relations of power that reinscribe institutional racism. Of course, for all of my intentions of the type of change this research should effect in teachers generally, the teachers in this study will have a major and active role in determining if and how the change that occurs in their professional lives.

Therefore, a very important implication of this approach on my role as a researcher relates to what happens to this research when it is finished. Denzin (2003) asserts that performances are pedagogical. On the textual level, the researcher still does have the last word when the research appears in academic journals or books. In this way, the research can help the researcher's career and hopefully might even advance the researcher's discipline in a substantial way. However, another goal of performance ethnography is to challenge the dominance of textuality, or as Conquergood (1998) puts it "the hegemony of the text" (p. 25). A performance approach challenges ethnographers not only to take information they learn from their research and write it in scholarly journals or books. The transformative effects of the research need to be more immediate. So, it is important that their work becomes pedagogical in various ways that text alone cannot achieve. While the work of this study ended up as text in a dissertation, scholarly journals, and this book, and while it may make an effective commentary on the field of sociology of education, I also hope the research act affected the thought and practice of the teachers I worked with. I hope they came to new understandings and practices regarding traditionally marginalized students. Equally important, I hope I have been similarly affected by the research, and I believe I have to at least some degree. I have come to new understandings of teachers and students and of my research and teaching practices. These new understandings have helped me find new ways to work towards antiracism in education, particularly in how I discuss race in critical conversations as a teacher educator and researcher.

Interviews

The data collection for this study consisted of open-ended, ethnographic interviews with seven high school teachers. Data collection consisted of two to three rounds of formal interviews with each participant and informal follow-up conversations with three participants. The initial interviews lasted approximately one to two hours each. These initial interviews were intended to explore the teachers' conceptualizations of colorblindness and perceptions of race and racism. While the research began with a set of research questions,[13] the research design was flexible and emergent, which allowed me to react to the conversational flow of the participants and to follow pertinent topics of conversation as they arose. At the end of the initial interviews, each participant was given one or two articles,[14] one that explains the basic tenets of CRT (given to every participant) and one that discusses whiteness and colorblindness (given to the first two participants only). As the study continued, the conversations around the CRT article were more relevant to the dialogues I was having with teachers, so I discontinued using the second article. The second interviews were conducted at a later date after the participants had read the article(s). This second round of interviews included a discussion of the articles and a reexamination of the conceptualizations of colorblindness and perceptions of race and racism.[15] These interviews lasted from one to two hours. I conducted a third interview with two teachers. These teachers and I felt that we had more to discuss with each other. Each of these interviews lasted approximately two hours. In addition, with all of men and two of the women, I had several informal interviews, ranging from 5 to 10 minute conversations over coffee to half hour discussions, often at their schools (when I was there to meet with my student teahers). After transcribing the tapes and typing all of the handwritten field notes, I ended up with approximately 300 pages of typed field notes.

Four of the teachers were women and three were men. Interestingly enough, the men wanted to be interviewed in a group, and in more social settings (i.e., at a cook-out and at a bar), and I conceded with their request. So, while I took notes and tape-recorded each of the interviews with the women, I was able to tape record only the first formal interview with the men. For the second interview with them, I only took field notes. In later chapters, I will discuss the affect of the different setting on my conversations with the male participants and will examine the very gendered nature of my interviewing and analysis.

Dialogic Performance

In the interviews, I specifically employed a dialogic performance (Conquergood, 1985) approach. It is a way that the researcher balances commitment and detachment. A dialogic performance positioned me squarely as a participant in the study in a way that also made me acknowledge my position and power as researcher. Because the teachers and I were co-performers of a dialogue on colorblindness, whiteness, and race, I was not detached from the meaning making that took place. The aim of an ethnographic approach that involves dialogical performance is to "bring self and other together so that they can question, debate, and challenge one another" (p. 9). Through the use of ethnographic interviews in this manner, I attempted to co-construct new understandings of colorblindness, whiteness, and race that the teachers (other) and I (self) arrived at together. By encouraging open conversation and debate, dialogical performance both acknowledges the distinctions between researcher and participant as it also challenges those distinctions.

In some ways, I adapted Conquergood's (1985) conceptualization of dialogic performance, maintaining some aspects of that approach and changing others. Following a dialogic approach very strictly, I would have let the teachers control the direction of the study more comprehensively. For example, all of the teachers in the study and I agreed that racial disparity is an issue in schools. On that point, we were on the same page about the key issue to be addressed in the study. However, some of the teachers and I had different opinions about the causes of that disparity. My main concern was that white teachers are unintentionally complicit in institutional forms of racism that promote that disparity. One way these teachers maintained this complicity is by adhering to liberal forms of antiracism. So, one of my goals in this study is to use the interviews to move the teachers to adopting more critical approaches to antiracism so that they can challenge their complicity in the unintentional, institutional racism that leads to disparity. By pushing the teachers in this way, I maintained dialogic performance's allowance for differences of opinion, but I also challenge a traditional approach to dialogic performance in that I came up with the agenda of challenging liberalism and colorblindness. My ultimate goal was to positively affect the academic success and schooling experiences of students of color, and in attempting to achieve that goal, I both worked with and against the teachers' motivations when I interviewed them. I did, however, at least attempt to balance the ways I challenged them by adhering to dialogic performance's commitment to also learning from the participants. Specifically, I tried to pay attention to how the teacher could inform me about how to frame the existence of colorblindness and the potential solutions to racial disparity.

Data Analysis

I analyzed each of the interviews according by using CRT to name whiteness as I discussed above. In addition, I looked at each series of conversations for both what they say about the interconnected topics of colorblindness, whiteness, and race and how they say it. To do this, I viewed each encounter as a performance. I looked at both the performative (what identities we performed) and the pedagogical (how the teachers and I came to new/different understandings) aspects of those encounters. So, in addition to examining teacher thought and practice via CRT, I drew Fuoss' (1997) articulation of the three dimensions of contestation that can be used to analyze cultural contestation in cultural performance—the direction of effectivity, the modes of effectivity, and the spheres of contestation—and I specifically used the first two in analyzing the dialogues of this study.

The direction of effectivity refers to whether a cultural performance supports or adheres to dominant ideology (i.e., ideology that contributes to domination) or whether it resists that ideology. Fuoss (1997) uses Thompson's (1990) articulation of ideology in describing the direction of effectivity.

> 'Ideology involves ways in which meaning serves, in particular circumstances, to establish to establish and sustain relations of power which are systematically asymmetrical—which I shall all relations of dominance. Ideology, broadly speaking, is meaning in the service of power' (Thompson, 1990, p. 7). In his view, ideology involves a culture's production, circulation, and reception of symbolic forms that either establish or perpetuate relations of dominance. (Fuoss, 1997, p. 84)

Thus, ideology as I use it in this book means liberal ideology as a dominant form of ideology in schools.[16] The direction of effectivity refers to whether the teachers' performances of racial understanding either supported or resisted that liberalism. The modes of effectivity, then, refer to the more specific *ways* in which those teachers' performances either supported or resisted that ideology. That is to say, the modes of effectivity were the articulations teachers used to either support or resist liberalism and how they used those forms. To reiterate, in my analysis I describe how the teachers' and my performances of the meaning of race and cycle of racism supported or resisted interpretations that rely on liberalism. I explore the specific ways in which we did that, focusing on the personal understandings that we each employed when we negotiated the meaning of race and our complicity in the existence of racism. In addition, I interpret how each of us made use of the interview itself, since analyzing the different ways that participants perform interviews can be pedagogical to how they and I also perform our understandings of race and racism. Using the analysis of the direction and modes of effectivity helped me interpret how liberal ideology interferes with more critically antiracist understandings and practices.

In each set of interviews I looked at how our explications of racism and complicity shifted (i.e., how we came to new understandings and how we may have advanced or regressed in our articulations) and how we contradicted ourselves. These shifts and breaks were the places where the performances were particularly pedagogical. Focusing on these breaks both between and within our rationales/logics—what McIntyre (1997) calls "'aha' experiences that emerged in the research project" (p. 658)—helped to determine the direction of the interviews and offered me a chance to deepen the dialogue that I had with these teachers. It was in these fissures where the teachers and I could challenge and inform each other. These "aha" moments helped structure my representation of the interviews as well.

Data Representation

In the following chapters, I present and interpret the dialogue I had with each teacher. In a certain respect, I present each teacher as a character in the overall performance (i.e., this research study). I discuss what the dialogue with each character says about the related concepts of colorblindness, whiteness and race (i.e., each character's frame of reference about these topics) and include the role CRT played in that dialogue.

I present these performances in a series of chapters. Some chapters focus on a single teacher. In other chapters, I group two or three teachers together as the "aha" experiences I encountered in discussions with each of them were similar. In Chapter 2, I present two of the teachers, Stephanie and Melissa. These were the earliest interviews I conducted, and my analysis of those conversations focused on how these conversations help set the stage for the rest of this study. Through my talks with these teachers, I learned some of the main issues relevant to white teachers' conceptualizations of race, especially the complex and non-static nature of colorblindness. Conducting and analyzing these conversations helped me gain insight into how white teachers both adhere to and contradict colorlind and liberal accounts of race and racism. In addition, it was these early interviews that helped me learn to articulate CRT in a more coherent way.

In Chapter 3, I present the conversation I had with Sarah, a young middle-school teacher. The focus of this conversation was often Sarah's attempt to understand the sticky issue of race. So, as I analyzed these conversations, I realized that much of the dialogue involved me learning how to play the expert about the issue of race and education. Sarah did not challenge my viewpoints very often. Rather, she wanted to gain a deeper understanding of how to deal with her own complicity in racism, especially via white privilege. Therefore, she challenged me to articulate my own racial understanding, something I think I learned to do in more nuanced ways because of my conversations with Sarah. In addition, Sarah's dialogue highlights the complexity, ambiguity, and contradiction involved when race conscious whites try to address their own complicity. In effect, the conversation with Sarah helped me understand how CRT could be used a dialogic practice.

In Chapter 4, I present my dialogue with Elizabeth, a veteran middle school teacher and proclaimed feminist who demonstrated a contrast to Sarah's desire to learn with a desire to debate and challenge. That is not to say that Elizabeth neither listened to new ideas nor wanted to promote more race conscious pedagogy. I believe she, indeed, wanted to promote racial equity as a teacher. However, more than any other teacher in the study, Elizabeth challenged my opinions and assertions. In part, her opposition seemed to stem from her feeling that teachers are not respected (especially by academics and politicians) as professionals who already attempt to address racial inequity. It also stemmed from her views on what counts as racism, views which both adhered to and countered liberal accounts. Interestingly enough, Elizabeth greatly enjoyed the interviews, an enjoyment that seemed to come from her stated pleasure of debating issues related to teaching. I also believe the dialogic nature of the interviews positioned her both as an intellectual and a professional, which she believes to be major characteristics of a teacher. As Elizabeth and I displayed a mutual respect and comfort in challenging each other, this is the interview that I believe best illustrates the notion of co-performing in a dialogic performance manner and it is an example of actually using CRT as a dialogic practice.

In Chapter 5 I present Elijah, John, and David, three high school teachers whom I call The Boys. I present them together primarily because they preferred to be interviewed as a group. Many of the issues of the other chapters—e.g., the presence of liberalism—existed in these interviews but to a lesser extent. Two of The Boys, in particular, were highly racially conscious teachers and they spoke frankly about their recognition of their own racial privilege and their attempts to combat that type of privilege in their practice. What I gleamed from these conversations was their performative nature. The Boys and I very much positioned and narrated ourselves as racially conscious educators (in effect, disassociating ourselves from the many white teachers, whom we consider not to have the same worldview that we do). So, in some ways, analysis of these conversations helped me understand my aspirations as a race worker/social justice educator more deeply. In addition, my dialogic style in this chapter was distinct from the other chapters, and this was in part due to gender. Even though I would describe each of the women in the study as confident in their opinions, especially Elizabeth, I felt it more difficult to challenge The Boys, and I believe I let the fact that we are of the same gender affect my style of interaction. I will discuss how this interview was different from the others in Chapter 5, pointing out and critiquing the particularly performative and gendered nature of that dialogue.

I conclude the study in Chapter 6. In each of the narrative chapters, I will discuss what the conversations taught me about how to being a critical methodologist with regard to the examination of race and racism. In Chapter 6, I sum up what was learned, examine the pedagogical nature of the study in more general terms, and point out the implications for empirical research in sociology of education more specifically. In discussing what CRT can offer to sociological research, I bring the discussion back to the implications for how the field represents and interprets its findings. As I focus on the pedagogical aspects of the study (i.e., what we learned and what can be learned) as well as its limitations (i.e., what is still left unclear or unresolved), I will also discuss more in more detail the practice of dialogic performance.

NOTES

1. Even though Morrow is specifically critiquing Denzin and Lincoln's (1994) volume, *Handbook of Qualitative Research*, the implication is for the field of qualitative studies in sociology of education more broadly speaking.
2. Giroux (2001, 1997) and Popkewitz (1998) are few examples of comprehensive arguments.
3. Greene (1995) gives a good example of this type of legal decision in his discussion of the Wards Cove case. In this case, Justice White did not require a cannery employer to change his racist hiring practices as it would be an unfair burden to the employer to devise a hiring scheme that lead to a more racially balanced workforce.
4. See West's (1991) *The Ethical Dimensions of Marxist Thought* for a thorough explanation of the use and purpose of theory and theorization in this manner. Stemming from Marx, West explains the goal of social research to be theorization (a contextual endeavor) rather than philosophy (an enterprise used more with the search for truth than for material consequences on people's lives).
5. Valenzuela (1999) is a notable exception.

6 Valenzuela actually helps mediate a disagreement the teacher and the students have, and her framing of the discussion within the larger institutional practices of the school helps them overcome their impasse to a large extent.

7 See Villenas (1996), Murrillo (1999), and Urrieta (2007) for examples and discussions of how researchers use the research act to work against the marginalizing racist practices that affect the participants of their studies.

8 She does want to raise their consciousness about their participation in white racism but also admits to focusing on how "*the participants* make meaning of whiteness" (p. 37, emphasis in original). In fact she discusses in depth the difficulty of being a white researcher attempting to critically analyze white racism with whites.

9 Giroux (2001) actually does make this claim but, at the same time, he also stresses the importance of the Frankfurt School.

10 See Guinier and Torres (2002, pp. 67–74) for a full description of the policy and its development.

11 Bell (1995/1976) makes this argument, which even goes back to the work of DuBois (1935).

12 I use this term in a similar way to Frankenberg (1993), who defines whiteness as "a set of locations that are historically, socially, politically and culturally produced and, moreover, are intrinsically linked to unfolding relations of domination" and argues that naming whiteness "displaces it from the unmarked, unnamed status that is itself an effect of domination" (p. 6).

13 Research questions (with probes) included:
A) What does it mean to be colorblind? Is it a practice that you adhere to? Do you employ it in your classroom? If so, in what ways? What are the benefits of being colorblind? What are the drawbacks? To what extent is taking a colorblind approach to matters of race supported in your school?
B) What opportunities are there in your classroom for discussions of race? How frequently do such conversations occur? If they do occur, how is race talked about by your students and yourself? How is Whiteness conceptualized?
C) What are your perceptions on racism? To the best of your knowledge, what could you say about your students' perceptions on racism?

14 Ladson-Billings, G. and Tate, W.F. (1995). Toward a critical race theory of education. *Teachers College Record*, 97(1), 47–68. Sleeter, C.E. (1993). How white teachers construct race. In C. McCarthy and W. Crinchlow (Eds.), *Race, Identity, and Representation in Education*, 157–171. New York: Routledge.

15 Research questions with probes included:
A) After hearing/reading about critical race theory, what is your initial reaction? What parts of the theory ring true for you? What parts do you not agree with? What about the theory confuses you?
B) After hearing/reading about the critique of colorblindness, what is your initial reaction? What part of the critique rings true for you? What part do you not agree with? What about the critique confuses you?

16 Though liberalism is not necessarily the major view of education held by the teachers in this study. Rather, it is the ideology that acts on teachers via the structures of schooling.

CHAPTER 2

SEEING EVERY STUDENT AS A TEN

Critical Race Theory and the Spirit of Colorblindness

> My personal philosophy of teaching is what affects all other things. The idea of being color is not my foundation. My foundation is that I try to see every student as a 10, a 10 in terms of potential, and so from day one I don't want to know what people think about my students ahead of time. I want to give to every student. I don't like to know how they did last year. I like to give them a chance from day one. I let them prove themselves or not prove themselves. I think that students should be given the opportunity to change. I know I've changed. I want students to reach their full potential in my class. That may be idealistic, but that's where I'm coming from. – Stephanie, 10th grade English teacher.

One of the challenges I faced in this project was how to critically question teachers—challenging their notions of colorblindness and privilege—who do attempt to promote socially just pedagogies and who do want to work towards racial equity. This was certainly the case with Stephanie, who I admired for her desire to want the best for all of her students—to treat them each as a 10. She had high standards for all of her students and went out of her way for struggling students. At the same time, I also find aspects of the above excerpt problematic. I do not think teachers can afford not to take a student's academic, experiential, and racial background into consideration. Stephanie acknowledged this herself.

> Ben: Do you think that people of color experience racism and face other impediments that may affect their performance?
>
> Stephanie: Yes, and I think African American teachers would say that African American students are at a disadvantage because they are minorities…I think that it is true that African Americans face obstacles that white students don't.

Stephanie never claimed to be colorblind. She acknowledged the obstacles that African American students may face and claimed that her students' racial backgrounds were important to their identities and behaviors. However, Stephanie still adhered to colorblind ideology in certain ways. Her example points out how complexly colorblindness can exist. It is sort of a moving target. So, my early interviews in this study—with Stephanie here and with Melissa, who I will also discuss in this chapter—taught me that simply labeling teachers as colorblind (or privileged or racist) is not an accurate or useful way to challenge colorblindness. Rather, these first two interviews helped me understand how the CRT practices of naming whiteness and property analysis could be used *in dialogue with* teachers, and that this dialogic approach was more valuable in challenging colorblind and liberal ideology. However, it was difficult for me at first to employ this dialogic approach. What was challenging was figuring out how to present my critical analysis of the teachers' ideologies in a way that also showing respect for these teachers as both professionals and allies in combating racism in education. I maintained the position of expert throughout much of the study, and especially in these first two interviews, in that I am the one who wrote up the narratives and interpretations and ultimately decided on the interpretations I have presented. Also, in these two interviews much more than with the later interviews in the study, I followed a more traditional research model in the interviews with these women—extracting "knowledge," experiences, and stories from the teachers—rather than fostering a more fully open dialogue. However, the instances of give and take that did occur the my subsequent analysis of the interviews did at least inform me of how to use CRT in dialogue and to then follow a more dialogic approach in the future interviews.

In addition, I did at least try to temper my expert status. I went into these interviews with dialogic intent, with the sensitivity that the teachers could challenge me and I may learn something in the process. To reiterate Conquergood's (1991) term, I attempted to enact this research study with the teachers being co-performers. Therefore, I often present the dialogue in this chapter in discussion format. That is to say, I present much of the conversation in the order it occurred during the interviews so as to convey the trajectory as well as the content of that dialogue. My intent is that the trajectory of the dialogue will be educative because it will show the give and take involved sustaining a dialogic discussion on race. Furthermore, my presentation of the dialogue sets up how naming whiteness and whiteness-as-property analysis used in a dialogic approach can move teachers from liberal to critical understandings of race and antiracism. I present the issues that exist in teachers' dispositions and actions, the complexity and contradictions of those issues, and how I learned to how CRT could be used to examine those issues. So, the two main missions of this chapter are to uncover the complexity of color-blindness as it exists in teachers' thoughts and actions and to illustrate the potential of CRT in pursuing more critical forms of antiracism.

Before I delve into those undertakings, however, I introduce the two teachers, Stephanie and Melissa. In some ways, these teachers were similar. Both were young, white women in their second year of teaching; both graduated from the same, prestigious Masters in Teaching (MAT) program of a prestigious southern university; and both were English teachers of regular and honors high school English. There were also some differences in the contexts in which these teachers work. Stephanie taught at a magnet high school in a mid-size southern city. The population of the school was 60% African American, while most of the remaining 40% was white with very small percentages of Latino and Asian students. Stephanie taught honors and academic 10th grade English, world literature. Melissa, on the other hand taught in a high school in a nearby college town (the same town where she completed her MAT). The racial breakdown of the students in Melissa's school was about 71% white, 16% African American, and 6% Latino with the rest of the student being from other racial groups. Melissa also taught 10th grade English, a combination of honors and academic level courses.[1]

More importantly, these teachers differed in their thoughts about racial disparity. Specifically, while I believe both teachers aspired to racial equity in their practice, Melissa seemed to believe in and embody a practice that adhered more closely to the key tenets of CRT (though she did not use the terminology of conceptual framework of CRT). This is not to say that there were no aspects of Stephanie's practice that also promoted racial equity. Rather, Stephanie's comments did seem to stem more from a liberal ideology that espoused colorblindness and failed to recognize and white privilege. So, while both wanted to know more (in general and from me specifically) about how to be more racially equitable in their practice, Stephanie had more questions and hesitations about how this could be accomplished (as came out in her comments about "the system") while Melissa saw more possibility of how to conceptualize and potentially enact a more critically antiracist practice.

CRT was valuable in highlighting both the questions/hesitations that Stephanie had regarding how to alleviate racial disparity and the potential for change Melissa's comments offer towards that aim. So, with CRT as the analytic frame, I use Stephanie's comments to illuminate the issues at hand and then Melissa's to put forward possible ways teachers can address these issues.

UNCOVERING COLORBLINDNESS AND LIBERALISM

Giroux (1997) asserts that the liberal ideology that dominates educational discourse de-politicizes culture. As this discourse does not recognize that power is linked to specific types of culture, it does not see schools as culturally dominant institutions. Therefore, it also posits that issues of culture—such as racism—that exist in schools to stem from outside of the institution of education. As the discourse does not acknowledge the racial (and potentially racist) aspect of the institution in which it functions, liberal interpretations of race and solutions to racism rely on colorblind arguments.

Simply put, being colorblind means not seeing a person's race or color. In education this plays out in the practice of not taking into consideration students' racial backgrounds when teaching them, grading them, or responding to their behavior. Teachers who adhere to colorblindness may say that they do not see color or that they treat all students equally, regardless of racial background. Both Stephanie and Melissa disavowed being blind with regard to color but adhered to this concept of equality.

> Stephanie: Yes, I think 'think that people of color experience racism and face other impediments that may affect their performance.' … I think that it is true that AA face obstacles that white students don't.

> Stephanie: I probably don't overcompensate for the disadvantages of minority students, which is, in terms of the students you get, there are white students who have disadvantages and they don't get more.

> Melissa: I work very hard to treat kids fairly. I know that minority students face challenges that white students don't. Saying that none of that matters isn't true.

> Melissa: I'd say that I'm reaching out…but I don't give the [minority] students anything that I wouldn't give other students.

These quotes show the contradiction inherent in their views of colorblindness. That they wanted all their students, regardless of racial background, to succeed is what I call the spirit of colorblindness. I see this as a positive viewpoint. It resonates with ideas of caring (Noddings, 1992)[2] and can even resonate with the idea culturally responsive teaching of promoting academic success and high standards for all students (Ladson-Billings, 1995). At the same time, both teachers recognized that students' racial backgrounds could affect the obstacles they face in educational settings. When these ideas of colorblindness come into contact with pedagogical practice in public school settings, teachers respond in different ways. I will show how these teachers responded in ways that both supported and resisted the liberal ideology that promoted colorblind interpretations of the reasons why their minority students were not performing as well as their white counterparts. I start with Stephanie because she was the first teacher I interviewed and because it is the interview that has most clearly illustrated for me the issue and complexity of colorblindness. Specifically, Stephanie's comments exemplify many of those that I have heard from the pre-service teachers I have worked with. They illustrate the liberal interpretations that many teachers use to understand racial disparity.

Stephanie was a 10th grade English teacher. She taught AP, honors, and academic level courses, and admitted that, despite minority students (primarily African American) representing 60 percent of the school's population, she had only a handful of African American or Latino students in her honors or AP courses. As my following discussion will show, Stephanie was a teacher that thought about the racial disparity she saw in school, desired to do something to address that disparity, yet adhered to aspects of liberal ideology that may have actually hindered how she could address the issue. As I stated above, my dialogue with Stephanie uncovered for me the complexity of and contradictions inherent in a colorblind viewpoint.

Here, I present one interaction I had with Stephanie. I show this extensive excerpt of our dialogue for three reasons. First, it again shows the contradictions inherent in colorblind views. Second, it highlights the connection of such colorblind views to liberal thought. Third, it offers an opportunity of where I could name the whiteness of Stephanie's thinking, which is one step in combating colorblindness. I will explain each of these points after the interaction.

> Stephanie: I do have more issues with tracking. I see that…I think that the way the school system is set up…how can it not be a problem? The fact that there is no real diversity in our honors and academic classes.

> Ben: Why do you think this happens?

Stephanie: The system is already set up. I do think it's largely tied to parent involvement. Parents who can get involved with pushing student to do well…"Are you doing your homework?" "You need to do well in school." It's a value. So they want them in the higher classes. Now does that mean that the majority of students in the standard classes who are African American—does that mean that their parents aren't as involved and don't care as much? No, that's not what I mean. What I'm saying is that something is flawed in the system.

Ben: Would you advocate for detracking?

Stephanie: I think that I lack experience to say that at this time. My first year I would have said, "Definitely," and then after a year of teaching a basic class where students, where it was behavior [issues]—I spent at least 50% of the time dealing with behavior problems. I mean students with IEP [individual assessment plans] and talking back, and of course I could have done a lot of things differently as a new teacher, but I think that I lack the knowledge and experience to answer that questions. I think that if we could integrate some students—from standard to honors—it might work but if it was an equal mix, I don't know.

In the above interaction, Stephanie was hesitant to be seen as placing the blame for in-school segregation on minority parents—i.e., she did not want me to think she believed that African American parents did not care as much—and at the same time, she in fact placed blame on these parents and students for African American students not being in honors courses. The students' own behavior was what made them ineligible for honors courses. So, Stephanie recognized that racial discrimination existed in the form of in-school segregation. However, she did not recognize the racial dynamics of how African American students were kept out of honors courses. Rather, she placed blame on an abstract idea about the institution of schooling—the "system"—that had no actors intentionally keeping certain students out of certain classes. The system was what was at fault, and Stephanie failed to recognize the specific institutional factors that caused this system and how these factors discriminated according to race, among other things.

This failure to recognize the discriminating dynamic of institutional factors is exemplary of liberal educational thought. In a liberal interpretation of racial inequality, there is no way the institution of education could be preventing racial integration, especially not intentionally since schools are basically value neutral with regard to culture. Therefore, Stephanie found the only visible reasons for the lack of integration of African American students to come from the students and their parents themselves. In this view, if the parents could change the way they motivated their children and if the students could behave differently, perhaps integration would be possible. Also, integration in this view could only occur if it did not dramatically challenge the structure of the institution as it currently existed. Stephanie could see some standard students being put in honors courses, implying basic students could not be integrated. In addition, the standard students could be moved up only if an equal mix of honors students remained in the class, insuring that there were enough of the right kind of students who could guarantee the current nature of the honors course be maintained.

INTRODUCING CRITICAL RACE THEORY

It is in this type of conversation with Stephanie where I began to see potential in naming whiteness—naming the whiteness of the institutional norms of the "system" and interrogating Stephanie's white way of labeling student behavior. One early instance of when I tried to challenge Stephanie's adherence to a liberal interpretation of racism was when we had a discussion of what thoughts or actions counted as racism. Stephanie saw racism very much in the intentions of the actor. She saw teachers as people who were for the most part trying to help and care for their students, so the language of racism felt very strong to her. The following part of this conversation came after Stephanie read an article on CRT in education:

> Stephanie: [School] is flawed in a way that gives advantage to whites. CRT would say that whites have constructed it that way—not that everyone want to keep minorities down, but that they want to keep that privilege.
>
> Ben: But you think that whites don't have that intention, so they aren't racist?
>
> Stephanie: But I can see how… I guess I could be swayed in some way to agree with what you said. I think that there are some gray areas here.

At this point with Stephanie, I just began to see how I could question what I saw to be a contradiction in the liberalism of Stephanie's thinking, so I tried to expose that contradiction. A little later in this discussion we revisited the definition of racism:

> Stephanie: [The article] says racism is not a series of isolated acts. I found that to be a very strong statement and perhaps it should be called discrimination, not racism. Discrimination to me means inequality where racism connotes conscious acts.
>
> Ben: CRT would argue that racism is not just conscious acts but it is part of it. Institutional racism, structures of society like schools, and processes of school like tracking, if they have consequences that systematically hurt minorities and favor whites, those institutions are racist in their outcomes. People benefit from the system and play a part in the system by supporting it.
>
> Stephanie: That makes sense to me.
>
> Ben: Do you think the institutions of school, such as tracking, are racist?
>
> Stephanie: I'd rather say it has racist outcomes.

Stephanie and I at this point still may have had some disagreement in our definitions of racism, but I also got the sense that she was deepening her sense of what the "system" actually was. I felt that shc was thinking through the issue that an institution actually has actors that at least perpetuate the norms of that institution and that the system does not have to be constructed the way it currently is. In a rudimentary way, by naming the white privilege that exists in institutional norms, I was helping Stephanie begin to envision a different way of thinking within such an institution.

I want to note that despite our disagreements on the definition of racism, Stephanie was always open to my questions. Her openness allowed me to begin to examine what I saw to be liberal and colorblind views. It also helped me feel comfortable in questioning her on her perception of behavioral norms. For example, several times in our discussions, Stephanie either mentioned or alluded to African American students giving each other a hard time when they would do well in class (e.g., she mentioned that they would comment to each other that they were acting white if they performed well in honors courses). In addition, she talked about the students in her standard classes, most of whom were black, as "not wanting it," i.e., they did not want to do well or try in school. Interestingly, she did acknowledge that there might have been something in the structure of honors classes that prevented students from succeeding. "No one, white or black, wants to be in the atmosphere of honors classes." However, she still placed the blame for why African American students were not taking honors classes on their behavior and on their parents' lack of desire to influence that behavior.

> Stephanie: I came in wanting to have the same high expectations for both classes [honors and academic], but the problem is when you have students who don't want it. I think the barriers are in the system, but also one of the things we hear from teachers is that we are here to help the students, but how can we do that when they don't respect you, they give you discipline problems. At least fifty percent of the time [in the standard class] was on discipline issues, fifty percent, so I think there is not only a responsibility for the system but for parent involvement.

In these types of cases, Stephanie did not acknowledge the ways in which students' and parents' past schooling experiences and current school practices may have influenced how minority students and parents may have been responding to schools. At other points in our discussion, she indicated that she thought the English curriculum did not represent African American culture and that more African American teachers were needed because they would be able to help African American students in ways white teachers could not. So, even though she did believe that school curriculum and personnel did not represent the culture of African American students, quotations like the one above indicated to me that Stephanie had not made the connection between discipline problems and this lack of representation or other school practices. Here, I am not making a causal claim about representation and discipline. Rather, I am trying to show that teachers' assertions (as exemplified in Stephanie's comments) about the barriers to equal education for minority students are at least partially rooted in liberal interpretations about the nature of public institutions and of racism.

I attempted (and unsuccessfully I believe) to work Stephanie through a whiteness-as-property analysis of school tracking practices.[3] I explained how white students may have more access to curriculum that represents their culture and how teachers assign whiteness to students who follow certain patterns of behavior. As I discussed in the first chapter, when teachers assign whiteness in this way, they help certain students access more rigorous curriculum because those students are deemed as able to handle it. I discussed this idea with Stephanie but failed to do so in a detailed way. I believe that one of the reasons my attempt to use this analysis with Stephanie was unsuccessful was that I did not have good examples that illustrated the specific ways in which teachers affect equal access to education because of how well they perceive their students to adhere to white norms. Stephanie's reaction was that my argument was interesting, but that was all. I do not think she could see how this process actually happens, something I was still in the basic stages of being able to do.[4] Interestingly enough, an early motivation for this study was to ground CRT in the work and lives of teachers. This agenda, though realized to a certain extent by the end of the study, was more difficult to work out initially.

Revisiting Stephanie's and my conversation on the definition for racism for a moment, I do want to show how I believe that property analysis can help teacher educators work with teachers to name whiteness, something I was not able to do at the time I interviewed Stephanie.

> Ben: You hesitate to put the label of racist on [the school's tracking practices].
>
> Stephanie: I guess if it was designed to have those outcomes, then yes, those who created it were racist and maybe that is the case. But because, at this time, and with all of the teachers I see who are trying to make a difference…I am more hesitant to say. I would agree that it has racist outcomes and that the system is racist. So if one would define not consistently seeking a way to change a racist system as racist…[5]

At this point, Stephanie trailed off, commenting that she is unsure about how to define racism. I asked her what other teachers might think, and she admitted to being interested in learning about this. Stephanie believed that most teachers really want to make a positive difference in the lives of their minority students and I agree with her. However, I think teachers betray this objective when they follow the kind of liberal, colorblind interpretations of racism that Stephanie exhibited in earlier comments. At this point in the interview process, I did not know ways to analyze this type of comment that would not make teachers like Stephanie feel directly and purposefully responsible for the racist outcomes their students suffer. However, in analyzing these types of comments using the tools offered by CRT, I began to understand how naming whiteness and whiteness-as-property analysis could be useful to respond to this type of comment. It could help teachers see the whiteness of institutions in their own actions, in effect enabling them to better address their own complicity in institutional racism without calling them racist. In the interaction immediately above, I might have been able to talk Stephanie through a property explanation of how teachers view certain students as being more capable and deserving because of how those students display behavior and knowledge that adhere more closely to white standards and how thus they, in essence, give those students better access to more rigorous and meaningful curriculum. We could have talked about how white teachers employ white ways of seeing to mark certain kinds of students as bright, gifted, "good students," etc. In using these labels, teachers may unintentionally support the segregation of minority students because the labels and, thus, contribute to the institutional racism of the school. In addition, it may have been my own preoccupation with Stephanie's and my different definitions of racism that prevented me from seeing property analysis as a useful tool at that time. I had not yet found a way to use property analysis to articulate the difference between liberal and critical modes of antiracism so as to work with Stephanie and accomplishing her antiracist goals.

LEARNING CRT

I now shift to my conversations with Melissa to examine how naming whiteness and property analysis be integrated into conversations with teachers, helping to challenge the liberal interpretations of colorblindness and race. My interviews with Melissa taught me how to use property analysis in a more useful way. While Melissa held certain understandings of racism that were similar to Stephanie's and while an adherence to liberalism at times was evident in her comments, Melissa was very critically astute about school practices that contributed to racist outcomes such as segregation. Together we were able to develop a more detailed understanding of how to name whiteness in school and teacher practices, and she helped me more deeply conceptualize how property analysis could explain the dynamic of racism in schools.

Melissa, like Stephanie, taught 10th grade English (world literature), and she also taught both academic and honors courses. The minority student population (primarily African American) of her academic courses more or less represented the minority population of her school, ranging from 10 to 15 percent. Meanwhile, in her honors courses she experienced the same phenomenon as Stephanie: she had two African American students in her three honors courses.

Melissa to an even greater extent than Stephanie recognized that minority students face challenges that white students do not. She also believed that teachers were responsible, at least to some extent, for addressing those challenges in school settings.

> Melissa: I know I've made allowances for minority students that I haven't made for whites. Society tells us that's not fair, but in my own philosophy it is fair, but in school and in the news you're told to treat everyone equally.

Here, Melissa did not equate fairness with sameness. Her concept of fairness was based in equity, not equality.

> Melissa: Everyone is not equal. It's unfair for a kid who has a private school background to be compared with one who has no [books] at home, no [resources].

In her teaching, Melissa tried to make up for these disparities the best she could. She discussed with me trying to get to know her students well, trying to reach out to them and their parents. She went to their sports games and attempted to understand them beyond her classroom, all of what she called "just good teaching."

However, like Stephanie, Melissa also had a tough time looking at teachers as responsible for/complicit in the racism in school. Her reservations about narrating teachers as intentional actors in this racism were based in her view of how much power teachers hold. After reading the CRT article, which does discuss teachers as those with power, she made this comment:

> Melissa: I had a little trouble with the idea that white teachers are the ones in power. I think that people who chose to go into teaching aren't the most powerful in society anyway. People who go into teaching aren't that privileged.
>
> Ben: Why do the authors talk about them as privileged?
>
> Melissa: It's not that they're not privileged, but they are specifically choosing a profession in which they are not going to be. So that throws a wrench. The argument is that people get power, they keep it, and they want more. But teachers don't have it. They are looked down on in society.

So, Melissa on the one hand recognized that schools, and many teachers, create circumstances that place minority students at a disadvantage, but on the other hand she did not see racial dynamic of how white teachers contribute to that disadvantaged situation. A discussion with her on whiteness as property helped us both understand how white teachers do in fact contribute to those disadvantages in a race-based way. What is interesting about Melissa's above comment about power is that immediately previous to that comment she stated the following:

> Melissa: I think most of [the article on CRT] is true. I think it's a specific factor in how [minority students] achieve and how they do in school. The most interesting argument is one about power, power that we have that we don't even realize. Thinking about education as a commodity—I agree with that.

So, while she may have had trouble seeing white teachers as particularly privileged and powerful—and I actually think she does make a good point about the career choice that teachers make and how teachers are viewed by society—she was open to thinking about how white teachers do, indeed, maintain an unrecognized form of power. This recognition helped lead us into a discussion of racial inequality in terms of property. As the following excerpts show, we were able to see and agree upon the ways in which teachers contribute to tracking minority students out of more advanced courses.

> Melissa: In a school setting, power comes through resources. One of the better arguments made [in the article] is that schools are not offering AP courses. I usually think of resources as computers, but white students are getting better classes, which will get them into college and get them better jobs. And get power.

This statement focused on inequity between schools, but it also opened the door to talking about how the same segregation occurs within schools.

> Ben: If it is whites trying to maintain power and access [to those resources], how is that done and how have you seen it done?
>
> Melissa: That was one of my bigger problems with CRT. I sat and thought about it but couldn't figure it out. 95 percent of honors classes are white and we've tried to change that. We've taken away all restrictions to get into honors classes—any minimum grades, no writing samples, just sign up. And we still have 99 percent of the classes—I have 3 black kids our of 75 honors students. I just don't know how it is being done.[6] I wish I could stop it from happening.

From here we got into a discussion of how this segregation may be done, or at least into how teachers may be complicit in the practice. We discussed how teachers view students in racialized ways and how this racialization in turn affects how teachers view minority students' abilities, how they advise on class choice, and how they give them access to more rigorous curriculum. We did not explicitly put this practice by teachers in terms of whiteness-as-property, but I think the following passage is an example of how teachers do, in fact, affect access to the commodity of education based on how white norms are privileged in school behavior. In responding to Melissa's previous statement, I asked Melissa about cultural and social capital.

> Ben: Do you see cultural and social capital playing in in any way?
>
> Melissa: I definitely think that is the case. I teach English and we are the only department that has honors, along with math. There are more minority students in 9th grade honors, and then they seem to drop out. And perhaps it is because the students don't have that discourse with the teacher, their grades drop and then they get discouraged from continuing. Because they aren't expressing their knowledge the way white kids are when they think, "Why am I bothering?' That's cultural capital, knowing how to play the game.

Introducing the concept of cultural capital to the discussion helped Melissa begin to see how school discourse—i.e., aspects of the culture of the institution of school—set up barriers to access. From here, Melissa and I were able to talk through how teachers support the liberalism inherent in this school culture, committing what Solórzano (1998) calls racial microaggressions.[7]

> Melissa: I think that there are things that we [teachers] are doing, not intentionally. I am a 10th grade honors teacher and other teachers try to help these kids, but being pretty rigid about what a high performing student looks like and acts like and produces is causing that kind of thing. I think that there are social connotations with those students that don't even have to do with the curriculum objectives. We prefer students who sit and raise their hands and

> don't talk, and we have this bias towards them even if we don't realize it. And I know from my reading that that's limited.

These comments have taught me to look at how teachers view students' behavior in racial ways and how they assign whiteness to those students who act in the preferred ways. In Melissa's interpretation, sitting and talking in the ways preferred by school personnel was in essence behaving in white ways, or ways preferred by whites. Teachers prefer those white ways of being and react to students according to whether they employ those ways of being or not. Furthermore, once teachers use white norms to judge behavior and academic performance, they allocate the resources of education more favorably to students who adhere to those norms, which privileges the students—usually white students—who come in with ways of being that already more closely match those norms. Those students become more eligible for honors courses or more rigorous work in the view of teachers. By leading Melissa through a racial property analysis of school discrimination, I was able discuss with her how teachers are complicit in institutional racism without instigating feelings of blame and causing her to defend her personal practice as a socially just teacher. She could see how there might be things that she says or does that may hinder minority students' chances at success in her class or affect their choices to attend honors or standard courses. The reasons why African American students in her school were not taking honors course might have been a little clearer to her.

What is interesting here is that I did not give Melissa any profound insight or knowledge. Most of her comments came from thoughts she already possessed. I just helped walk her through a property analysis of those thoughts. It is from this type of dialogic performance that I learned to more concretely see and better explain the property arguments that I already believed in. I could see how property analysis could be used to dialogue with teacher about complicity in racism. In fact, naming the whiteness of teacher practices and using a property analysis of teacher conceptions of student behavior and ability showed me how CRT could be used with teachers in order to create revisionist accounts of the causes of the racial disparity that exists in schools. Teachers like Melissa already carry these accounts with them. Dialoguing with Melissa using CRT as a guide just helped me bring out these stories and let us see them in a new light, a process that was easier than with many teachers I have worked with because of the degree of critical consciousness (Ladson-Billings, 1995) that Melissa already possessed.

For example, she recalled a conversation about 9th grade curriculum change in her English department (which had already done a lot to increase the diversity of author representation in the 10th grade curriculum):

> Melissa: There was a lot of resistance to taking off the white authors [from the 9th grade curriculum]. There are five required books. *Raisin in the Sun* is the only one by a black author—some considered *To Kill a Mocking Bird* to be diverse. Some wanted to replace *Animal Farm* with *Black Boy* and people freaked out. One guy went so far as to say that 70% of the literature would

> represent 15 to 20% of the population. I can't believe he had the nerve to say that.

Melissa had an understanding that this teacher in her department viewed literature written by black authors—like *Black Boy*—as only speaking to black students while those written by white authors—like *Animal Farm*—hold universal merit and can speak to all students. So, she already had a critical understanding of the racial dynamic of the curriculum as property and of how whiteness is seen as the norm—i.e., white ways of being are not seen as racial, so white authors can represent people from any race. Using the tool of naming whiteness—in essence calling that teacher's viewpoint for its white way of seeing—helped me uncover with Melissa how comments such as those above are rooted in a vision of whiteness as a form of property. We discussed how teachers, who are mostly white, have trouble giving up what they know. The way I interpreted and explained this practice to Melissa was that some white teachers are unwilling to give up their white racial advantage. This made Melissa explain it in terms of teachers' comfort zones.

> Melissa: I think the big thing is that [white teachers] are going to have to look at different standards in how things are done. Some of these teachers have been looking for the same qualities in a paper for 20 years. I think the fear is in not knowing and giving up your time. I think it's hard. The fear of giving up *Animal Farm* us the fear of leaning something new. There is a comfort in teaching something you are familiar with. And if you are not familiar, then it's a problem.

Melissa was careful not to portray teachers as intentionally discriminatory. She was sympathetic to the difficulty involved in teachers giving up what they are comfortable with, yet at the same time she thought change was necessary. By putting this conflict in racial terms in a dialogic fashion, Melissa and I were able both to avoid labeling teachers *and* to discuss the possibilities for teachers to change their unintentionally discriminatory practices. Melissa talked about attending seminars that focused on culturally relevant approaches to teaching and her attempts to alter the English curriculum, and her insights show how teachers can begin to work towards anti-racist approaches to education. Equally important, Melissa's discussion of these insights and possibilities helped me see the value of using CRT in dialogue with teachers and begin to put into words the possibility for change that such dialogue could offer.

CONCLUSIONS – BEGINNING TO UNDERSTAND

Despite the potential touchy topic of conversation and despite the fact that these early interviews did not involve as much give and take on the ideas as I had originally envisioned, overall the dialogue with both Stephanie and Melissa was fruitful. I was able to challenge liberal, colorblind interpretations of and approaches to antiracism and to begin to push them to develop a more critical form of antiracism, and I was able to do so without essentializing the teachers or promoting narratives of racist selves. I believe this dialogue became possible because of the respect I showed for each of the teachers as professionals and intellectuals. In fact, Melissa made comments of disdain for the usual ways in which school administrators approach equity education with teachers. She was disparaging of how administrators and non-educators (e.g., politicians, the public, etc.) did not view teachers as professionals. So, I believe the fact that I used a very dialogic approach in interviewing these teachers, in effect setting them up as professionals, helped me sustain a conversation in which we both learned. In less performative approaches to ethnography, interviews may lead to expert analyses of participants' words and much less attention may be paid to the pedagogical potential (for either the participant or the researcher) of the interview itself. In other words, the educative aspects of the study are left to the analysis and implications stages of the study and not the data collection process.

What I found as I interviewed these two teachers, reflected back on those interviews, and poured over the transcriptions was that these two interviews informed me on how to enter into and perform a research study that examines teachers' conceptualizations of race. This chapter, then, has been very much about what the conversations—what was said, how it was said, and how the conversations developed—taught me about how to use CRT to analyze views of race. Even more specifically, these interviews taught gave me a deeper understanding of naming whiteness and whiteness-as-property analysis. Before conducting these interviews, I understood both practices as concepts but could not apply them. These interviews showed me how they could be applied in dialogue with teachers.

In addition, these interviews helped frame the study in several ways. They taught me the complex nature of colorblindness in the views and practices of teachers, how colorblindness is attached to liberalism and how that liberalism exists in teacher thought and practice, and how teachers both are complicit in institutional racism and work against that complicity. Furthermore, analyzing these interviews pointed out to me that the study was as much about asking the teachers what they consider to be racism as much as it is an examination of colorblindness. In this regard, the teachers performed both ideological and counter-ideological understandings (in respect to liberalism as a dominant ideology) of colorblindness, whiteness, and institutional racism. I have showed the contradictions within and between these teachers' comments – contradictions that reveal the coexistence of perceptions that both adhere to and resist liberalism in its dominant ideological interpretation of racism.

Finally, though I could not articulate it with these teachers at the time, these two interviews helped me hone my intentions in the study. Specifically, they helped me recognize that my intent was to move teachers from liberal approaches to antiracism that rely on colorblind arguments to more critical approaches that recognize institutions as value laden in terms of race and culture. I wanted the teachers to acknowledge and use approaches that, like CRT, center race as both an ideological construct and a lived reality.[8] That is to say, I wanted to the teachers to address how race is a complex issue but one that is central to the nature of schooling.

So, these initial interviews were pedagogical to me in that I more deeply learned to articulate CRT and I began to see how to apply it to the practices of teachers. CRT helped me to uncover these contradictions and showed me its potential in countering some of the problematic aspects of liberal ideology. This process of uncovering and challenging the ideological undercurrent also served the aim of teaching me how to "see" in a more material way the analytical tools of naming whiteness, property, and revisionism, tools that became valuable for me in future interviews and in my own teaching.

Discussing examples of classroom experiences with both teachers enabled us to name the many ways whiteness existed in school practices. This naming helped us revision (i.e., reinterpret and reframe) those experiences in more racially conscious ways. Furthermore, dissecting the way teachers assign and control curricula based on whiteness helped me get a better hold on what property analysis can do in teacher education. Melissa's understanding of how teachers use students' cultural capital to assign them certain standards of whiteness helped me provide a response (at least in my thinking) to Stephanie's labeling of students as not wanting education based on her observations of those students' behaviors. Even though I was not able to challenge Stephanie's labeling in these interviews to a great extent, what I learned from Melissa about teacher practice has provided me with a new way to work with my own pre-service teachers. As I stated earlier in the chapter, Stephanie's comments are similar to those I hear from many students in my education courses. The discussions in this study were concurrent with a course on social foundations and multicultural education I was teaching. I found that they helped me talk with my students about how teachers' conceptualizations and labeling of their students—i.e., as either "good students" or as "needy" or "disrespectful" students—was linked to how these pre-service teachers used standards of whiteness to judge their students. That is to say, the pre-service teachers' use of white norms to judge their students affected their perceptions of those students' desires and abilities.

The reason this property analysis has become so useful to me is that it offers a language that counters the specific modes of effectivity that teachers may employ to support liberal interpretations of racial disparity. For example, when Stephanie labeled students as "not wanting it," she was viewing the school structure as culturally equal for all students, regardless of their racial and cultural backgrounds. Such labeling supports liberal interpretations of institutions such as schools as value-free. Property analysis has helped me learn how the modes of effectivity that support dominant ideologies exist in practices such as labeling. Furthermore, this analysis has helped me uncover and thus explain to white educators how such modes of effectivity make us complicit in institutional racism.[9]

Of course, my big failing at the time of these initial interviews, especially with Stephanie, was that I had not yet thoroughly developed that language that could help me explain this complicity. With Melissa it was not as much of a problem because of the critical racial consciousness she had already developed. Therefore, my inability to be as dialogic as I intended to be did not affect that conversation as much. With Stephanie, however, I was so focused on analyzing her comments according to the tenets of CRT that I did not focus enough on how to work with her more dialogically and take advantage of her liberal racial consciousness in order to promote more a more critical approach to antiracism. In Chapter 3 and 4, I will discuss how I learned to develop and use CRT as dialogic performance. In Chapter 3 especially, I will explain more of the insights I gained about CRT in this way. There are aspects to CRT that make it fit very well with dialogic approach, and I will discuss the value of this approach to me as a teacher educator.

NOTES

1 I use the teachers' terms for the hierarchy of course levels, which are from "highest" to "lowest": advanced placement (AP), honors, academic, and basic. The term academic was recently adopted at both schools to replace standard—i.e., non-honors—courses.

2 I do not go into a discussion on caring or culturally relevant pedagogy, as they are is not the focuses of this study. I do think, however, that an examination of the nexus between caring and antiracist practice could prove very fruitful for teacher educators. Tapping into teachers sense of caring may be a good entry point to promote racial consciousness as well.

3 This was really my first attempt to use property analysis outside of a being a student in a graduate course.

4 I will show what I believe to be better uses of property analysis later in this chapter and in future chapters.

5 I am reminded here of Tatum's (1997) analogy of institutional racism being a like a moving walkway at the airport for those have racial privilege. Even if whites do not walk, they are still carried forward, so the only way to not take advantage of racism is to actively act against it.

6 Here, Melissa's understanding is still rooted to an extent in the ideology of liberalism. The institution of schooling is seen as value-free. Since the explicit barriers to honors courses were removed, no barriers exist. Liberal thought in this way does not recognize the culture of the institution—i.e., discourses and ways of being exist that privilege some and discriminate against others.

7 Here, Solórzano draws on the work of Pierce, Carew, Pierce-Gonzalez, and Willis (1978); Davis (1989); and Delgado and Stefancic (1992). He summarizes the work of these scholars by defining racial microaggressions as the "subtle and covert ways" in which whites exhibit racism towards minorities. The participants in his study commented that these forms of racism had the effect of them "feeling out of place," encountering "lower expectations," and feeling "invisible."

8 I will explain these ideas of race more when I present my interviews with Sarah in Chapter 3.

9 This analysis of labeling becomes very important in my conversations with Elizabeth, presented in chapter 4.

AN EQUAL OPPORTUNITY PUSHER

Using Critical Race Theory to Deepen Racial Awareness

> ...In terms of being colorblind it's sort of funny... we have a school vacation for a week or two weeks, and I come back and I'm like "Oh yeah, a lot of my students are black." When I'm teaching for months I don't even notice that, and when I'm away and I'm on vacation and am around a lot more white people then all of a sudden I become aware of "Wow, I'm in a school of a lot of African Americans!" And I don't even notice. And when I see pictures developed, too, of like school trips and my class, I go "Wow, there are a lot of minority kids!" and you know it's just interesting. – Sarah, middle school math teacher.

Sarah was an interesting person to interview. As I will show, like Stephanie and Melissa she had a complex view of colorblindness. In a later section of this chapter I will explain how that colorblindness played out in her thinking and practice. The comment above, for example, shows that she claimed some sort of blindness with regards to phenotype. At the same time, her thoughts on whites' complicity in institutional racism (including her own complicity) challenged this blindness. These thoughts were key in Sarah already promoting a critical approach to antiracism. So, before talking about her conceptualization of colorblindness, I will discuss Sarah's astute understanding of complicity.

Sarah taught middle and high school math at a public charter school (Phoenix School) in a mid-sized southern city. While she lived in the same predominantly white college town as I did, the city where the school was located had about a 45% African American and 45% white population (with the remaining 10% of the population being primarily Latino). Before teaching there, Sarah taught middle school in the college town, but despite the experiences of many white teachers,[1] she preferred the city school and was effective there.

> Sarah: Part of the reason I left tutoring to go into teaching was that I didn't feel like I didn't get to help African American students. I had all these rich white kids coming to my house for $45 an hour. I felt I was so good at doing that [math tutoring], that it let me help different people who can't afford me... And I've had great result in terms of my tests, end of year tests. The first two years at Phoenix, 100% of my kids got 70% and better – Algebra 1, Geometry and Algebra 2. This year I had one kid fail Algebra and three fail Geometry, on the EOC. I lost my perfect record. [Laughs.]

Though the exact numbers of the racial breakdown of her students varied from class to class, approximately 80% of her students were African American and this fact seemed to increase a racial awareness she already possessed.

It is also important to note that I knew Sarah before I interviewed her. About five years before the study, her husband and I taught ESL together for one year. So, when first talking to Sarah, I often wondered in the back of my head what his thoughts would be on what I was saying. I knew some of his views with regard to race and education—views that were similar to mine in some ways and different from them in others. As the interview progressed, however, I quickly got wrapped up in our conversation. That may be in part due to the fact that Sarah was a rapid-fire speaker and was very intense in conversations. She put all of her energy into them and asked hard questions—for the most part because she really wanted to learn more. In particular, she wanted to know a lot more about racism, including the ways that she could be more racially equitable.

As I stated, Sarah already had a keen understanding of whites' complicity in racism in education (not to mention in society in general). It was something she had thought quite a bit about. Like me, she already carried with her the belief that all whites have racism.

> Ben: Is colorblindness a good practice in regard to race, and is it a practice that you adhere to?
>
> Sarah: I think it's an ideal to strive to. I don't know that everybody reaches it. I think it's important to be colorblind, but I don't know if in practice everybody is.
>
> Ben: What about *anybody*? Do you think that anybody is?
>
> Sarah: That's like saying is anybody completely without racism. I think that people might like to say that they are but I think it's very ... it's almost impossible that anyone truly is... that anyone is truly without any sort of their own racism, even if they don't want to admit it themselves.

Her views on colorblindness exemplified the spirit of colorblindness, what Stephanie might call seeing every student as a 10—as I will show shortly—but more than with any of the teachers I interviewed she also acknowledged her own role in perpetuating racism and wanted to resist liberal ideological interpretations of that racism. In this sense, she had Melissa's same sensibility of the racial microaggressions that whites commit unintentionally. She often asked herself about the racial dynamics of events that occurred in her school and in her own interactions with students. Even when she became tempted to divert conversations about race to a discussion of class, she used that same self-critique to acknowledge the important of race.

> Sarah: On page 50 [of the CRT article], when it's talking about inequality, race is the central construct of understanding inequality. I guess I still wonder...isn't inequality also caused by class? There are poor whites and there are wealthy blacks. Um...I guess I would say still, my gut would say, it

is primarily race, but I feel like…I don't know…I guess that class should be talked about also as being like the second biggest factor to inequality.

Ben: Um, yeah it's interesting…

Sarah: And I don't know if they even were feeling like…I don't know if it even… it didn't really address when there are you know wealthy… I guess it's just myself, I mean I grew up middle class, lower middle class, I had a lot of financial aid…like I know there are wealthy blacks that I met that were not on financial aid, so I saw you know… I mean I'm not poor, but then there are a lot of poor whites who never make it to college, and there are some wealthy blacks who do go on to get MBAs and go to college, but I think it is… I mean it's not as prevalent…

Here I really got the sense that Sarah was trying to work out for herself her internal conflict in thinking about race versus class issues. It seemed to me that she was hoping our conversation would help her work through such conflicts. So, I feel like we had similar beliefs on how much race contributes to inequality, and that she was using our conversation to work out an articulation of those views in order to make them more clear to herself, let alone to others. This was a real "aha" moment for me because these interviews did the same for me with regards to CRT. They helped me use CRT as a resistant mode of effectivity (i.e., a way to resist a dominant ideology) against colorblindness and liberalism and then to also articulate to others how CRT could be used in such a fashion. I will revisit this latter idea when I discuss dialogic investigation later in this chapter. For now, I will explain how CRT helped us better discuss race in way that resisted liberal ideological interpretations. For example, our conversation about the race versus class issues helped us explain to each other the importance of centering race:

Ben: Um…What I often ask in my scholarship is that, it's—relating this back to feminist theory and social class theory—when people do feminist theory, [I feel] they are rarely asked, "Well why don't you also do class?" And when people do social class theory, [I feel] it's rare that people say, "Well you can look at race there." …Maybe it's changing now, I don't know. But when you talk about race theory, about centering race, and from whites especially…

Sarah: They say, "Why don't you do class?"

Ben: And [CRT scholars] are not saying class isn't important, but they're saying…

Sarah: Race is primary.

Ben: In race scholarship, race is central because you can't explain—like if you do studies of students or property—social class doesn't explain everything. There are still more people [of color] that suffer the consequences, even if you control for class. So I think that's what they're saying.

In trying to work out a response for Sarah on why CRT centers race, Sarah was able to fill in the gaps in my articulation. So, not only was our discussion on the centering of race educative for her, it was also educative for me about how to more deeply understand and then articulate the need to center race in analyzing school inequity. In essence, much of what my dialogue with Sarah turned out to be was to help her gain a deeper understanding of *how* whites are complicit (for the most part we already agreed that we are). That is to say, she wanted to understand more deeply how racism and complicity happen so that she could work better at challenging them in her practice.

Sarah was easily able to center race in reflecting on her practice and professional experiences. Sarah was especially astute at recalling interactions—both those that involved herself as well as others—questioning the racial dynamic of those interactions, and trying to understand how they might include examples of racial discrimination. One example that shows her willingness to question the racial dynamic of an interaction was when she described her school's director's attempt to push students to get their GED rather than continue on to get their high school diploma.

> Sarah: I worry at school. I feel like it's happened a lot, but then again our school is very much minorities [i.e., predominantly minority students], so it's hard to say is it happening because of that or because we have poor students—you know if you have poor whites is the same thing happening—but I feel like our director a lot this year and last year really encouraged a lot [of students] to drop out and get GEDs, when they were like 16 or 17 and they were still in 8th grade or 9th grade. But I don't know if that's because they are African American or…

Even though Sarah did not know if the director was suggesting the pursuit of the GED for these students because they were African American, she was willing to ponder the racial dynamic of his thinking. In the end, she was not nor could not be sure, but what is important about this comment is that she was trying to understand the racial aspect of this type of practice by a white educator. Similarly, Sarah also acknowledged her own feelings of racism that she carries with her.

> Sarah: …when I think about my own racism—everybody has it—driving around in certain parts of the city [that have large percentages of African American]… just driving around back roads of the city, I sometimes do want to make sure the windows are rolled up, the doors are locked, and I feel like more scared, and I'm aware that it's a minority and not really with poor whites, I'm aware that I'm having…
>
> Ben: So, you're saying that you notice more in a poor black neighborhood than in a poor white neighborhood.
>
> Sarah: Yeah. So, then I start to think that I feel a little more racist and a little guilty clicking it [a door lock] if I'm going by somebody [who is poor and black].

> Ben: So it sounds like you are saying that you don't have negative feelings towards black people, but there is something that makes you think.... So what you are saying that it [racism] is a little more broad than just intentional.
>
> Sarah: Exactly. Right.

Sarah acknowledged—at least at some point—that her actions were based in assumptions about people from different racial background, and she was willing to question those actions and the racial dynamic of her assumptions.

This type of self-questioning opened up Sarah to considering actions that might actually counter complicity. Later in the same part of our conversation, we discussed part of the CRT article by Ladson-Billings and Tate (1995) where they explain using race as an ideological construct. In that section, the authors discuss Omni and Winant's (1993) argument that race cannot be looked at only as either an ideological construct (i.e., a social construction) or an objective condition (i.e., a material reality). I attempted to explain what the authors are trying to say,[2] and Sarah's response again showed her willingness to consider an example of potential institutional racism and how one teacher [a colleague of hers] attempted to combat it.

> Sarah: I just had a huge question mark at the bottom of page 48. I did not understand that part at all. It talks about is race an ideological construct or an objective condition, or an epistemological—you know that whole paragraph I was just like confused.
>
> Ben: [I spend some time looking over the paragraph]. Okay, so it's saying that if it's an ideological construct...I think what they mean is if it's only a social construction—like it's all in our heads, that we've created, that if you believe that that's all it is—it has no real reality, that you ignore how that construction is actually affecting people.[3] I mean biologically there's no such thing as different races. We're all part of the same sub-species—things like that—so it doesn't make any sense biologically. However, socially, we have lived realities and it has effects that are material, such as whether a student is punished or not, or who historically has been able to own property, all of these types of things. So, even though it may not be a hard reality—what they say here is an objective condition—it still has some material effects. So, you can't think of it as purely a social construction. You can't think of it as pure reality either because who counts as black and who counts as white, it all falls apart in this sense, because people are mixing, races aren't clearly...
>
> Sarah: I see what you are saying, I see... It made me think that in terms of racism, there's panic a lot about the kids, of their race being wrong. Like a lot of times it'll have a little box on a standardized test. It'll say black, and they'll be, "Oh, no, no, no, I'm mixed race," and they'll be "Look, they made a mistake here on this one, it says I'm white, but I'm black,"... it bothered them, and also there were questions about, "Did you parent go to high school?" "Did your parents have a college degree?" all these surveys that they do. One teacher who is white, I thought this was great, he brought up that kids go into these tests feeling bad, like "Oh wow, here I am checking

I'm black, I'm checking that my parents only have a high school education or 8th grade education, and now I'm going to take this OG test," you know, knowing that this person next to me may be checking that my parents have a PhD. And they feel bad about this going into the test… [so he decided to] do this the day before the EOGs [End-of-Grade tests].

So, my attempt to explain that race is socially constructed and that as a construction it also has material consequences helped Sarah think of an example of how the construction of race affects her students.[4] She saw that the designation of race on standardized tests and students having to mark their race may have induced in them what Claude Steele (1997) calls stereotype threat. Furthermore, in her example, Sarah was able to think of actions that potentially resisted the racist outcomes, such as stereotype threat, that marking race may cause. I do realize that it is certainly difficult to know to exactly what extent Sarah's colleague was able to counter the stereotype threat his students may have been feeling, but in focusing on Sarah's understanding of this event, I do believe that she was able to see how teachers are a part of a system (as Stephanie might put it) that re-inscribes racial "realities" and therefore imagine possible response that counteract potentially racist consequences. Discussing an article on CRT—and specifically the CRT tenet that race is constructed in ways that privileges those raced as white over those raced as non-whites thus reifying white privilege—helped Sarah develop her own worldview about the existence of racism and then to possibly use that worldview to resist liberal interpretations of how to counter discrimination.

As we continued our dialogue on the existence and reification of racism in society in general and in education in particular, we were able to use discussions of property to more deeply understand the construction of white privilege.

Sarah: Okay. On the next page, top of 58,[5]…does this mean that there's so much in terms of bad experiences that have affected Americans that in order to feel better about their own superiority…?

Ben: Yeah, or anything. Even if we find the status quo reasonable as whites—I took the test, I got this score, so I deserve to be in this class; or I took the test, I didn't do as well, so I don't deserve to be in this class—without looking at the bias of the test, the lack of resources that may have affected how I study for the test, the history of being in schools before then. So, if we don't look at that critically…

Sarah: In terms of …

Ben: Oppression becomes rationalized. They deserve to be in those classes because of x, y, and z…they didn't take the test, they didn't do well.

What I was attempting to do in the above interaction was explain how in using the structures of schooling as they currently exist, people actively take part in the segregation of students into different classes. Certain students are viewed as having earned a place in higher-level classes, so school personnel assign them to those classes. I wanted to show that a history of access to resources, or denied access as the case may be, has affected students' current placement in schools. This in turn affects their current access to educational resources, such as certain types of curriculum. Sarah's questioning about a specific part of the CRT article—a part of the article that explains how whites maintain privilege and how counterstories can disrupt the justifications of that privilege—helped me better understand and begin to articulate to myself how property analysis can help explain the active maintenance of white privilege. Likewise, the interview setting allowed me to begin to explain it to Sarah. I still had a long way to go to make that argument more coherent, but the dialogic nature of the interview gave me a place to start to see how property analysis could lead to revisioned explanations of racial disparity, explanations that resisted the dominant liberal interpretations.

COLORBLINDNESS REVISTED

To open this chapter I presented a quotation from Sarah in which she discussed times when she did not notice or forgot people's skin color. In fact, she brought this up more than once.

> Sarah: I know myself that I'm so not visual. I feel like there's been some moments where there's been people that I couldn't describe and I can't remember if they're white or black. I feel like that's happened once or twice. That I was kind of like, wow! ... You know what it is, when somebody comes to the door, when there's a random stranger sometimes coming to visit or see somebody [in my class], there are times when I don't remember if they were white or black. And that has happened a couple times. I remember thinking, "Oh, that's kind of weird," like that I'm so non-visual I don't even notice that... It's not something when I see them more than once, but if briefly a parent comes to the door, or something, and if I say, "Someone came by yesterday for you," and they ask, "What did they look like?" "I can't remember. I don't even remember if they are white or black." I remember saying that at some point, and thinking...more criticizing myself, thinking, "Damn Sarah, you're so non-visual that you don't even remember that!" [Laughs.] ... But I think a lot of it is that—especially when I'm at Phoenix for a long time—that I get used to the norm being that everybody's black and that the exception is that sometimes somebody is white.

I got the sense from Sarah that her experiences of forgetting people's skin color were accurate, that she honestly did forget color at times. However, the last part of her comment above is important, that she did notice color when it was related to difference. For example, she did notice color when it is the exception:

> Sarah: Because it is four out of my five classes that are majority African American and just the one seventh grade pre-algebra class... And it wasn't just... I did think in my head, "Oh, that's interesting, the class that had the most whites was my hardest class behavior-wise." I did have that thought.

She noticed, and admitted to noticing, when students' behavior did not fit her expectations of racial behavior. Again, she did notice habit of categorizing student behavior according to racial preconceptions and called that into question. I was not sure what to do with this part of our dialogue at first. It was and still is hard for *me* to imagine not noticing a person's race, but Sarah was so honest about her own ideas on race that it is also hard to imagine she was lying to me. In analyzing this conversation, I began to explore in new ways how different forms of colorblindness might exist. Maybe Sarah exemplified a certain type of visual colorblindness (i.e., a colorblindness based on phenotype or racial appearance) versus a cultural colorblindness (i.e., a colorblindness based on some sore of understanding of behavior as related to ethnicity). Perhaps visual colorblindness, the claim that she often did not notice a person's skin color, was linked to how she saw colorblindness as a goal. She believed a person's skin color should not matter for their chances at being successful in school, for example. Our extensive dialogue on the topic did bring out that same sense that Stephanie had of a spirit of colorblindness.[6]

> Sarah: I will say that I'm an equal opportunity pusher. I'm really pushy with all my kids in terms of getting them all to succeed. I don't know that I'm conscious of it, but thinking of how I try to equally get kids of all races to come for help at lunch or after school or equally calling all parents trying to get everybody on board to raise their grade. So anybody who has Ds and Fs, I'm on the phone pushing.

So, regardless of race, Sarah was going to push her students to be successful in class. However, Sarah went back and forth about how much she noticed a person's skin color or race. In the same part of a conversation, she explained that she judged students on their math performance alone and then immediately described how that student's race made her think about her decisions with that student. For example:

> Sarah: When I try to decide in terms of moving kids in math class, moving them up a level or down a level based on how they do on the placement test…I think I'm very careful to make sure that I'm… I'm really just looking at the numbers. [I note that she is struggling a bit about how to express this]. I'm not at all concerning myself with somebody's race. I'm looking at how they did on the test, how they've done on previous tests, how their records look. You know I don't know that I'm really thinking about…because my school is majority minority students. That's sort of my… people stand out more if they're white in terms of race, but I don't know that I'm thinking about that. I did think that toward the end of this year there was one kid who did very poorly, he started off pretty good and then he did really poorly and he was one of the few white kids we have, and I ended up not moving him down, and I didn't even ask myself, "I wonder if by chance…" [alluding to the fact that she made this decision because he is white.] It did go through my head [later] that I had somehow partially thought he is smart enough to handle it. I actually had those thoughts later but then I looked at the numbers and I thought, "Well, his numbers were in the 80s, they were with people that

I kept in that level," but it was interesting that I actually thought about it [that decision not to move him ad the possible racial factors in that decision].

Ben: So, you might not have thought about it at the moment but you did later.

Sarah: Right.

At first, she claimed that race was not a part of her thought process at all, but when she reflected on whether or not keeping the student in the same level class, she did call the race-less-ness of her decision into question. Like with Stephanie at times, I saw colorblindness as somewhat of a moving target – sometimes it meant one thing and sometimes another. This movement in the concept furthered our conversation.

Ben: So it sounds that you are saying is that the way you strive to be colorblind is by relying on test score performance or homework score performance, academic performance. Is that correct?

Sarah: Yeah [hesitantly], and I guess I'm more treating kids on other ... are they trying... in my mind it's always interesting... in treating the other students—but it's very mixed up on what their race is—are they doing their homework, are they raising their hand, are they behaving in class? I feel like I have strong students and weak students of every race.

Sarah here adhered to some version of a universal ideal of a good student. That is to say, in the above comment, she put forth a vision that there is a way to behave in class and, furthermore, the way of behaving is not related to race and applies to all students. This vision of the universal good student was supported by other comments she made and may have been connected to her desire for all of her students to succeed—her spirit of colorblindness. This is what she said when I ask her about the advantages of colorblindness:

Sarah: Oh, I always think it's a necessity that when we're treating everybody equal and we're not coming in with preconceived notions of "well in my experience Hispanics and Black student don't do as well" [she says this part putting on another person's voice], if you have these racist thoughts then you're going to put that on the child and not grade them fairly and it's going to be a self-fulfilling prophesy. I think it's really important that you don't [do that.]

When I then ask her about the drawbacks to being colorblind, however, she resisted the notion that a universal proper way to behave existed.

Ben: Do you think there are any drawbacks to being colorblind?

Sarah: Well, okay, here's one. I guess that the shouting out—I read *Why are all the Black Kids Sitting Together in the Cafeteria*[7]—and that sometimes culturally African American students shout things out instead of raising their hand, and if you have the white model of you-have-to-raise-your-hand-if-you-wish-to-speak, then you might not realize that some of these African

American…it's cultural that they're shouting out and it's not that they should be penalized by this white code of ethics of how you should behave in the classroom. So, if you're aware of, okay they're black, you know tolerating different behaviors.

So, along with having some colorblind notions of what it means to be a good student, Sarah also practiced a kind of color consciousness. She wanted to take students' racial backgrounds into consideration when reacting to their behavior in the interest of equitable treatment. The above comment led us to talk about the importance of noticing difference. Like with Stephanie, I noticed a contradiction in Sarah's belief in the ideal of colorblindness and her insistence of the importance of noticing racial difference. So, like with Stephanie, I attempted to dialogically question Sarah on this contradiction so as to focus on how noticing (or not noticing) racial differences can affect students' access to quality educational experiences.

Ben: This sounds like that there are cases where you believe in colorblindness, however, would in that type of case it not be important to notice difference?

Sarah: Right, like I'm saying in that case it would be important to notice differences.

Ben: Do you think it's possible to notice differences and be colorblind?

Sarah: Yeah [assuredly]. Yeah, yeah, yeah.

Ben: …You used the phrase "treating everyone the same." If people have different behavior patterns, how do you treat everybody the same? I guess what I'm asking is what does treating somebody the same mean to you?

Sarah: Having the same high expectations for achievement. [Pause.] Academic achievement or…behavior. Having the same high standards

Ben: So, if you have the same high expectations of behavior, does that mean you have the *same* expectations of specific behavior? [Pause on both our parts.] What I'm trying to get at is you make it sound like you realize that it may be a cultural phenomenon that black kids may shout out more and that to them in certain circumstances that may not be considered bad behavior.

Sarah: Right.

Ben: But in some other code of ethics that may be.

Sarah: Right

Ben: It sounds like then that you have to have—even if you have high expectations—that you have different expectations.

Sarah: Right. Yeah. And I don't know that in practice I always do that. I mean I know Isaac [who is black]—and in that class of 15, maybe 11 were black, one Hispanic, and three white—but he, I just felt like as a person had trouble not shouting out and so I think I let him shout out more without getting as upset as I would with other students, who I felt like could not control it, but I don't think it was based on race. I think it was based on him.

So, our discussion moved again. In some sense I was trying to nail down Sarah's version of colorblindness and how it affected her practice. It seemed that, at times, what she thought to be the ideal of colorblindness did not always match up with her actual thought process or practice in class, but that at times she also did base those actions in some sense of what I have called the spirit of colorblindness. While she diverted the conversation away from race (articulating how she responded to students based on their individual personalities), difference—i.e., being cognizant of difference—was important to her in order to help her students to succeed.

Ben: It sounds like what's important is that difference to you is based on individual students.

Sarah: Yeah, it really is. I think I was thinking more of for other people in general, allowing for different behaviors based on race, but I guess for me myself it's…I tend to be much more strict, wanting quiet, wanting—whether that's a white value or whatever—wanting kids to raise their hand, but occasionally—I don't know why I picked Isaac, I taught him two years in a row—I felt like he could not control it.

She had an ideal of good behavior in her class—wanting quiet—but she was also willing to break her own rule about noise in order to be able to work with particular students. To put this in terms of CRT, she has a system of categorization that was in part racial but she was able to use her racial awareness to alter and question that practice. Her rules and her exceptions to them were not entirely based on race—the idea of caring about students despite or because of their differences may have also been important—but again she was interested in considering what was racial about them. She felt that considering this racial dynamic via cultural difference was important for her to be equitable as a teacher. Our conversation served as a way for her to work out how she could acknowledge difference in order to maintain that goal of equity. For example, she was very astute about how race may have factored into parents' involvement in decisions about which classes their students would be in.

Sarah: I was very much aware that Allison, [the director's daughter, who is white], I definitely wanted to move [her down a level], but he would not have her be moved. And Scott, who's white, I talked to his mom and he also ended up staying. And so like I was aware racial-wise that when I've called parents who are white and say I want to move the kids down, the parents fight me on it more, and there kids end up not moving down… And I remember that bothering me in a way because I was thinking that… I think culturally sometimes some African American parents may think, "Okay the teacher knows what's best, I'll just do what they're saying," versus some of the Caucasian parents thinking, "No, I want to move my kid up," etc, which may

> be based wanting the kid to have challenge or wanting the kid to be with more kids of their same race.

One important aspect of our dialogue was that my motivation in it was to get Sarah to see her contradiction. My adherence to the CRT ideal that colorblindness masks the categories—like good student, proper behavior, etc.—that whites have constructed and used to maintain white privilege, resisted the liberal ideal that categories exist or can be created that apply to everyone in the same way. I believe Sarah to some degree actually also adhered to that challenge to colorblindness and supported a more color conscious ideology, especially as she conceptualized difference. CRT was a motivation for me to draw this ideology out of Sarah with the hope that she might challenge those aspects of her thinking and practice that still adhered to liberal interpretations of the necessity of colorblindness. In the preceding excerpt, Sarah was aware of how cultural differences (as she saw them) could lead to different ways of accessing the structural aspects of an institution of education. She believed that some white parents might have a cultural and social capital that enables them to gain access to a certain curriculum. She did not use the term entitlement, but her comments hit on the possible senses of entitlement that white parents might have, and furthermore, she was willing to question the racial dynamic of that sense of entitlement—e.g., white parents might want to move their children so as to be in classes with more white students.

At the same time, Sarah both posited and resisted essentializations about black culture. At times, she commented that black students had more trouble raising their hands rather than shouting out. Even though she commented on this type of behavior to highlight how it is important for teachers to be understanding of different types of behavior because they may be valued by different cultures in different ways, she did essentialize black students as behaving in a certain way when she made these comments (and I notice that she did not do the same with white students). There were other times, however, where she commented on how such behavioral difference was an aspect of individual difference (versus cultural difference), e.g., with her student Isaac. She thought his tendency to shout out might not have been so much a cultural practice but rather just his individual way of behaving. Again, I was able to use CRT motivations to delve into what is possibly racial about the way she sees and interprets her students' behavior and academic performance.

Specifically, the CRT idea that institutionally sanctioned ways of categorizing students can lead to racial disparity helped me maintain an investigation of how even an antiracist white teacher such as Sarah can promote an ideology that potentially reifies white privilege.

> Sarah: I think I very much judge kids on intelligence, on how smart they are. One of the smartest kids is black and I think more about how brilliant she is and I know some white kids who are lazy. And I wouldn't say I have negative feelings about kids that are not smart but I think in terms of grouping in my mind [to understand how she thinks of her students for this research performance.]

> Ben: Do you think definitions of things like intelligence can be racial? Not racist but racial? Like when you talk about a white code of ethics or having a white understanding of something. Or do you think of that as more universal.
>
> Sarah: [long pause] I mean it might be a white code of ethics [her tone is very unsure/hesitant here.] I think of it as being more intellectual being doing hours of homework, getting good grades, but it's just uniform for everybody, but maybe that is just coming from my own definition.

In this interaction, I was trying to name the whiteness of what white educators may see as universal ideas, such as intelligence. I was using terms she had used previously in the interview—specifically "a white code of ethics"—to get her to challenge any adherence she might have had to a universal definition of intelligence. My questioning was motivated by my own conviction that beliving that categorizations such as intelligence can be univerersal masks the fact that those categorizations are rooted in whiteness. So, when she switched the conversation from intelligence to homework, I attempted to question a universal way of interpreting how students do homework.

> Ben: I mean I'm curious…because I wonder, too…if we judge student based on how much homework they do, maybe a student has more time to do homework or a different context…
>
> Sarah: For my grading, that may be why I do think of homework as being very different than…in my grading I don't count homework. They get different grades for effort and citizenship than for content. For moving people to the next class I use the content grade. It would be interesting to look however to see if whites got better grades for effort and citizenship. So I get kids who do really well on tests and quizzes but who may get low grades on effort because their homework is horrible. I've had some people [teachers] argue with me that that doesn't make any sense…My students can get good grades anyway because they're showing me they know the stuff.

I am not sure my questioning in this interaction ever got Sarah to understand the potential white quality of her views on intelligence or homework—an understanding I do think she was able to discuss at other points in our dialogue. She saw that citizenship may have a racial quality but not that content might as well. So, she relied on the content grade when moving students from class to class. However, she did at least recognize that context may affect student performance on homework, so she did not use that in her grading. She at least attempted to make her grading more equitable. Also, with homework she was willing to consider the possibility that whites may have been getting better grades based on contextual factors. The whites in her school tended to be wealthier than her black students so maybe they did have more resources to rely on and perhaps that did lead to them getting better grades on effort. So while I did not get Sarah to see categorization in the same way that I did with regards to intelligence, my contextualization of her decisions was an attempt to revision decisions that teachers make. Sarah did explain and think about how she attempted to achieve equity in her practice, and by discussing those attempts in racial terms, perhaps she was able to gain a deeper understanding of how race affects teacher decisions.

DIALOGIC INVESTIGATION AND CRITICAL RACE THEORY

I think it is important to remember that Sarah wanted to be more racially equitable in her practice. I attempted to use naming whiteness (such as the whiteness involved in categorizing intelligence) and some property analysis for us both to come to new understandings of how to work towards racial equity. Because of her desire to understand, more than with any other interview I was in the position of expert, of the one with the answers. While I took on this role to some extent with Sarah, I also tried to challenge it so our conversations could be more dialogic, so we both could learn. Interestingly enough, what I learned from my conversations with Sarah was a next step with regard to dialogic performance. From Stephanie and Melissa, I learned how to use some of the tools of analysis that CRT offers. I learned some of the ways that whiteness could be named in order to revision teacher thought and action that appear racially benign but that potentially contribute to the cycle of structural racism. I also learned from them how to analyze some of the ways in which access to property interplays with whiteness in classroom settings. Those conversations taught me about the usefulness of CRT in an analytical sense.

From Sarah, on the other hand, I learned how to take that knowledge of CRT and make it more dialogic, to use it to work with Sarah to delve more deeply into investigations of teacher practice and to come to more nuanced understandings of how the systems of categorization teachers use—to assign grades or judge intelligence, for example—can be racial and potentially causes of racial disparity. I believe that after our conversations, Sarah and I were better able to recognize liberal understandings of race and racism and articulate critical reexaminations of those understandings.

Furthermore, because Sarah and I were able to agree on the centrality of race and develop a way to articulate it, I was able to push Sarah on what I saw to be remnants of liberalism in her practice. I may not have always been successful in getting her to see the racial dynamic of all situations in the same way that I did, but we were able to go into detail about exploring what is potentially racial about them. So, while the conversations with Stephanie and Melissa were pedagogical about what CRT can offer to the examination of complicity in an analytical way, the dialogue with Sarah was pedagogical about how to focus that analysis—in a dialogic manner—on specific day-to-day details of a teacher's practice.

Sarah's questioning was a very important part of fashioning this dialogic investigation. Her pursuit of deeper understanding and a more coherent way to articulate that understanding were very useful for me in cultivating my own functional articulations of concepts relevant to CRT and race in education.

> Ben: Do you think he would consider himself to be colorblind? I mean, you may not know that.

Sarah: Yeah. I guess I'm talking about my definition. Could you tell me what you think the definition is of colorblindness?

Ben: The definition that I use and that most people in my field would use is that you either don't or claim to not see a person's skin color and/or you might see but you go out of your way not to treat people differently because of it. So for some it means that, people who say they're colorblind might say, " I don't even see color, I don't even notice." Others might say, "Yeah I see it, but I don't think about it, and I treat everyone the same." Might your director say something like that?

At times in our dialogue, I was lucid about articulating concepts, such as colorblindness, that are important in understanding racism and racialization. In excepts such as the one immediately above, I may not have articulated the most comprehensive (or even most accurate) definition but I did put forth a definition that captured some of the key aspects of the concept and one that was clear to Sarah. In addition, I was more or less confident that my definition did not counter those used in the fields in which I work (such as teacher education, sociology of education, etc.) At other times, I had much less confidence and much more difficulty in articulating the processes of racialization. For example, in the following excerpt Sarah and I discuss the definition of racism and about who can actually be racist.

Sarah: Yeah, but well then, what if they're black but they're a CEO of a company, and they're in a position of power? Then can they have racism?

Ben: Well, some people say they can have power and they can have prejudice but they can't really have racism, because even though they're connected—it depends—some people say yes they can. Some people say well if they have negative opinions of they're own group, then that's internalized racism. [I can't tell if I was just floundering to be careful or if I'm avoiding the question. Do I know the answer? This is big part of my interviews with Sarah. And I think it is interesting here when I am typing this up, that I am imagining potential audiences—like at conferences—where my opinions are out on the table!]

I wrote the bracketed notes above when I was transcribing the interview. As I show in this commentary on my own comments, I am unsure of the answer about possible actors in racism. I am also unsure of my position as expert on the subject. I imagine others in my field as cops in my head, to borrow a term from Boal (1992, 1995), policing me for my ideas and the way I posit them.

These instances of uncertainty were at least as important to the development of my understanding as the times when I was more confident in my comments. Whether my reactions were lucid or not, Sarah's questioning pushed my thinking on race and CRT. Her questions were not intentionally challenges, but they were direct questions that did not let me talk around concepts but rather forced me to explain them in specific terms. In other words, the honesty and openness of the dialogue pushed me to develop CRT as a mode of resistance in a more coherent way. I believe that this coherency is important in using CRT as a way to challenge complicity in teacher education settings. Our dialogue made me think of how I wanted to examine issues of race as a teacher educator in classrooms with pre-service teachers, and at several times in both my note taking and transcription I made side notes about the implications of my interview comments for me as a teacher educator. For example, I made the following comment when we continue our discussion on what counts as racism and who can be considered racist.

> Ben: Basically what I'm saying is that it all comes down to how you define racism. So, on some levels I'm more interested in what people think rather than us all agreeing on a definition of racism because I can't get us all to agree on a definition. In class I'll say, "Here's the definition I'm going to use." ... but in the end it becomes more of semantic argument, so I try to use other language to get at what people are thinking about what is racist... [Note: So maybe in class I should have students label and analyze situations according several levels and different definitions of racism—and they can use and defend their own definition later.]

In this last quote, I was really learning what I think is important about the word "racism" so as to combat discriminating practice, and in the bracketed section—which I wrote at the time of the interview—I was thinking about how I could use these ideas as a teacher educator. I could again envision an audience, this time the students in my pre-service education courses. I have heard the argument from these students many times that racism is an intentional act based purely on the dislike or distrust of the "other" and therefore anyone can be racist—whites, blacks, Latinos, etc.—and that there is no difference in the type of racism that people carry. At the moment of the interview, I could picture and hear these students and therefore imagine how the new understanding of racism that Sarah and I developed in the moment might be educative for me in how I respond to and work with such students. At times in the conversation, when I heard these students in the back of my head, I used the interview with Sarah to test out my ideas on how to respond.

> Ben: Some people might say, "well, if they have prejudices against whites, they're prejudiced, but still not racist because even though they have individual power, they don't have power because they don't have racial power. They have other power but..." So it really depends on the definition. [Note: I quote the imaginary person here – is that to save me from putting "my" opinion on the table...or is this my opinion?]

In this instance I was using the dialogue to help me be the "expert" on race in education. I imagined those various audiences—such as pre-service teachers—where this conversation may play out. In the bracketed section, I pondered the phrasing of my comment. Sarah's direct questioning about what counts as racism really made me focus on how I word such responses. So, I was learning to be an "expert" on race and a teacher educator. This was very performative research in the pedagogical sense.

In the end, my conversations with Sarah have made me think about how this type of dialogue can be used to resist the liberal ideology on race. I can test out responses to all of the cops in my head—e.g., students, race scholars, or book reviewers. I am also left wondering about how different viewpoints on colorblindness (e.g., as an ideal on the one hand or as an impossibility on the other) may support or resist liberalism in different ways and with varying degrees of effectivity. I still wonder how the particular articulations of colorblindness can potentially resist and/or support liberal interpretations of racism in education. I am also left wondering—but also hopeful—about how dialogic performance can be used to develop practices that counter such interpretations. I believe Sarah has shown some possibility in some aspects of her practice. Furthermore, using CRT to probe her thinking has enabled me to think more about how I can continue to examine and challenge categorization practices that lead to racial discrimination.

CONCLUSION

Using CRT with Sarah has helped me understand CRT as a theory. As a theory—rather than just another method to study race—CRT has epistemological implications. Race is not just another factor in disparity but rather a central focusing point of analysis. To center race in the analysis of (and eventual resistance to) racial disparity in schools means that the question, "What is racial about this?" must always be asked. With Sarah, this was easy because she was almost always willing to ask that question and we were able to sustain the discussion of disparity in racial terms. Drawing from Ladson-Billings and Tate's (1995) article on CRT, I was able to discuss with Sarah examples of how teachers' understandings of race and their categorizations of students according white norms could make whites complicit in institutionalized racial disparity. The resulting dialogue has helped me similarly sustain conversations on race in more difficult situations, such as with pre-service teachers in my classes. In addition, it helped prepare me for my conversations with Elizabeth, who was did not always agree that teachers' complicity was a leading cause of disparity. As I will show in Chapter 4, having had the experience with Sarah of centering a discussion of racial disparity on teachers' complicity became useful when working with teachers who resist framing their practice into such terms. In that chapter I will show how the analysis I developed with Sarah helped in the conversations with Elizabeth and will also show how Elizabeth helped me sustain this conversation with teachers who resist putting their practice in terms of complicity in institutional racism.

NOTES

1. Studies by Aaronson (1999) and Merseth, Mont, and Rees (1996) document the problem of teacher turnover in urban schools.
2. I explained the difference as I understood it at the time. Again, Sarah's direct questions about concepts from the article force me—on the spot—to articulate those concepts as if I am the expert in CRT (and race in education in general). By forcing me to articulate in this way, I learn through the study to put my ideas "out there," to see what I think about my articulation, and to re-conceptualize and solidify my understanding of race and CRT. I will explain this process more in Chapter 6.

[3] I really got caught up here with words like reality, hard, objective, condition, etc.

[4] Interestingly, this example also shows that thinking of race can also lead to thinking of other forms of inequity, in this case inequity related to educational background. This supports Guinier and Torres' (2002) assertion that politicizing race can lead to working against other causes of inequity as well.

[5] In this section of the article, Ladson-Billings and Tate (1995) are discussing the need for the use of counterstory to disrupt the rationalizations—such as a belief in meritocracy—that prevent whites from understanding or interrogating their own privilege.

[6] I actually told Sarah the story of Stephanie's comments about seeing every student as a ten at one point.

[7] Referring to Beverly Tatum's (1997) book.

CHAPTER 4

MOVING TARGETS

Racism and Responsibility

Ben: …when I talk about racism exists and racism as inherent, that doesn't mean that I think most white people hate black people, but I think ways society has been structured and I think it is in a large part whites have been dominant for a long, long time in society that those things happen that lead to racial inequality. [Through this description, Elizabeth often nods and says, "right, right," in affirmation.]

Elizabeth: So do I feel like that's a racist outcome?

Ben: Just tell me what you think about it.

Elizabeth: No I'm still thinking about it…[we both laugh]… Um… I think that that's a position…[still thinking]… I'll say yes keeping in mind that for me racism… racist is always more about the perpetrator than about the results.

Ben: So you do have somewhere in there that the word racism always has some derogatory [connotation that people are intentionally prejudiced]…

Elizabeth: I'm afraid I really do, yeah.

Ben: I'm guessing most people do.

Elizabeth: But I just realized I did. [She laughs.]

Elizabeth more than any other teacher I interviewed challenged me on what I considered to be racism and particularly on white teachers' complicity in it. She often fought my views of white teachers' complicity in spite of doing some of the very things in her practice that I think white teachers need to do to work against that complicity. I felt as if often her challenges came from her desire to do just that—to challenge and to argue, which were aspects of her personality that she openly admitted to. She also felt that teachers were not treated like professionals by either policy makers or academics, which made her weary of the critique of teachers, who she saw for the most part as professionals doing all they could to help their students. Her resentment of the lack of professional treatment was similar to Melissa's in that she did not like to be seen as un-intellectual.[1] She wanted to have a say in what the solutions to racial inequity should be and saw teachers as agents of equity. Her resentment was also different from Melissa's in that, while Melissa was more open to engaging with the teacher education literature or with teacher educators themselves, Elizabeth maintained her skepticism that researchers in teacher education could offer her anything but critique. This difference in response to academia could be due to the fact that Melissa was in her second year of teaching and much more close to the world of teacher education while Elizabeth was in her tenth, though I believe other factors, such as Elizabeth's enjoyment of argument as I mentioned above, were important as well.

These and other aspects of Elizabeth's personality also enabled me to challenge her back and helped me see some potential for movement in her thinking, especially with regard to how teachers are complicit in institutional racism. She considered herself a feminist, so she did not have a hard time seeing that some in society are put in less privileged positions than others. In addition, she was a very socially and politically conscious person in general. With regard to race, she often admitted to the white cultural dominance that exists in society even if at times she could not see all of its incarnations or the possibility of how teachers could challenge it. Her acknowledgement of white dominance did allow me to push her on seeing the ways that dominance rears its head in schools and the classroom. Like the other teachers in the study, Elizabeth's beliefs and practices regarding racial equity contained both liberal and critical elements. In my attempt to highlight and promote those more critical aspects, we got into very detailed and hearty discussions about what teachers could do to counter racial disparity.

Elizabeth's penchant to challenge what I said along with her respect for being challenged herself helped make this the most dialogic interview in the study, at least in Conquergood's (1985) sense of how a dialogic approach involves a give and take between co-performers. Elizabeth did not usually hedge on language, which allowed me to be more direct about naming complicit practice than I was with any other teacher.

In addition, and also because of her directness, I had to challenge myself to listen to Elizabeth when I disagreed with her (which was often) so I could learn her perspective more deeply and possibly leave myself open to changes in my argument. I also had to challenge myself to come up with articulate responses to her statements so as to potentially shift her thinking as well. I will illustrate what we both learned from this dialogue later in the chapter, where I will discuss how working with a research participant who was more prone to challenge my ideas on racism and complicity helped me develop more deeply the way in which I articulate resistance to the liberal interpretations of racism, and I will include the role of CRT in that process. However, before I go into those pedagogical aspects our conversations, I will present my interpretation of Elizabeth's views on colorblindness, racism, and complicity and will illustrate the dialogic nature of our conversations.

THE SPIRIT OF COLORBLINDNESS

> Ben: Have you heard the word colorblindness and what does that mean to you?
>
> Elizabeth: It means that when you look at or deal with someone, your primary thought about them has not been treated as a category. They're not necessarily white to you or black to you or Hispanic or whatever. It doesn't mean to me that you are unaware of that info. It just means that it's not any more relevant than the color of their hair.
>
> Ben: It's not so much that you don't see it, but it's just a physical feature.
>
> Elizabeth: Yes! [with affirmation but not overexcitement]. I guess that's more my personal definition of it.

Elizabeth, like most of the other teachers I interviewed had a complex view of colorblindness. At least as a concept, she understood it as being able to see skin color, but to treat people the same regardless of color. As the following excerpt shows, in practice she recognized that behaving differently with different people because of their cultural background could also be important in some circumstances.

> Ben: Do you see [colorblindness] as something as something as positive or negative or…
>
> Elizabeth: Yes, both. It's more like… It's along the lines that you don't want the negative aspects of racial stereotyping or racial experience to influence your behavior with the current crop of students, but you also do need to be aware that there are legitimate cultural, racial differences the same way that there are… that I would deal with a male differently than a female—in very minute ways. I might conceivable go into an interview with the parents of a Hispanic child differently than I would the parents of a black child different than the parents of a white child, but ideally I guess for me… it's not just that. It's what I know about the parents' interaction with me in the past—has that been positive or negative?—what I know about if they seem to support education or not.

She believed that racial and cultural difference, then, did matter in how she acted, for example, with parents. However, it was not only racial and cultural difference that mattered. Her interactions with these parents as complex individuals and not just as racialized subjects were also important to her. Thus, it seemed to me that Elizabeth understood that culture (and she was referring more specifically to race and ethnicity here) had an affect on how parents interacted with her, but that within specific cultures, individual variation also existed. Culture was important but not determinate.

Her last statement from the previous excerpt betrays another area of complexity and ambiguity that I observed in Elizabeth's understanding of race. She understood that a parent's way of interacting might be affected by their cultural background(s), but at times she shifted in and out of an understanding that there might be different acceptable ways to interpret behavior. In other words, at times she indicated that there may be different ways to show support of schooling and that these different ways could be based in part on racial and ethnic background and at other times she adhered to the idea that there was a "right" way to show such support. While I believe that most of the time Elizabeth seemed to understand that attitudes such as a support for schooling were affected by the interplay between cultural background and societal experience, comments such as the one above—"if they support education or not"—also indicated to me that there are times when whites may forget that interplay and how it affects people's reactions.

For the most part, however, Elizabeth was willing to do a lot to help her students succeed and her ability to do this was partially based on a sense of racial and ethnic equity.

> Elizabeth: If [the parents] speak English or not has become a serious issue. There's a Hispanic parent I know who speaks almost no English and one of the things that I am always willing to do is speak Spanish—and I know just enough to embarrass myself publicly—and I'm really willing to do that because then a lot of Hispanic parents get, "okay, if she's, the teacher, willing to embarrass herself, then it's okay for me to try and speak English now." And it doesn't always work but it often really helps the dynamic.

In cases like this, Elizabeth seemed willing to challenge her own comfort zones in the interests of her students and their parents. In addition, while Elizabeth was not always willing to leave her cultural comfort zone, her astuteness about her own whiteness did enable her to expand this zone in order to be a better teacher.

For example, we discussed the ways in which Elizabeth acknowledged the cultural differences of her students and tried not to judge them because of those differences. In one instance we talked about her articulation of the behavior of her Latino male students.

> Ben: It is interesting because you use the…word aggressive with the Hispanic males, as being aggressive towards women. And I don't mean to critique you, but I just mean to… is it a negative to you?
>
> Elizabeth: I think that is what I was trying to say. To me it did always feel very aggressive. I still feel like it is aggressive, but I understand that's because that's my culture speaking…But I realized about a couple of months into it that [how the students behave] is not my culture. I can't judge that culture, and I can't these people telling me things based on my cultural ideas of what is a good idea. So, yes, I do use the word aggressive, and I do mean aggressive because it felt aggressive, but at the same time it wasn't aggressive—except for the one kid who was being harassing—by a different culture. So, yes, that's what I mean.

For Elizabeth there were different ways of behaving appropriately that were based on the various standards of different cultures. She was able to bracket her own judgment about such behavior—she admitted it felt aggressive to her but also prevented herself to some degree from categorizing that behavior in ways that could lead her to negatively react to the students. In addition, I got the sense that Elizabeth was able to distinguish between an acknowledgement of different standards and a stereotyping of those cultures because of their difference. In other words, she recognized different ways to interpret what is acceptable may exist, but she did not assume that students and parents adhere to any specific interpretations. Rather, she related to her students and their parents as not only members of a race but also as complex individuals. In fact, it was Elizabeth's racial consciousness that allowed me to open up a discussion with her about what I saw as her partial adherence to a liberal ideology that viewed school standards as neutral.

In fact, I believe some areas of Elizabeth's thinking, if not always her action, adhered to liberal ideology. In particular, her beliefs about how certain dispositions and practices were linked to institutional racism and her opinions about possible counter-responses to that racism adhered to liberal interpretations. Yet, her understanding of the significance of racism was complex. She understood that whiteness and maleness dominate in U.S. society and that racism and sexism exist, but overt (rather than institutional) forms of those oppressive forces were at the forefront of her thinking when we discussed how to challenge those forces. It was almost as if the other forms—the subtle, insidious forms—were "the way things were," and that fact might not be desirable but "we" (meaning people in general) have to deal with it. Oddly, her pedagogy seemed to do more than just deal with it.

Thus, it seemed to me that there was some contradiction in how she articulated the existence and various manifestations of racism. She knew that she was born into a racist society and with white privilege, but because it was so dominant and prevalent, there was not much that could be done about it. In addition, at times she said it was racist to ignore and not acknowledge that dominance and privilege, but at other times she thought that calling such ignorance racist was going too far. In the latter instances, she seemed to indicate that if people did not intentionally oppress people, they were not being racist even if they did not do anything to challenge their own privilege. This intentionality was important to Elizabeth's conceptualization of racism and I tried to draw it out.

> Ben: It sounds like your conceptualization that school is somewhat this neutral place.
>
> Elizabeth: I think structurally schools and on paper schools are neutral places but of course since they involve people… I mean I could never dispute like what you asked earlier which is that are teachers teaching equitably… I mean some teachers don't, some teachers are racist or sexist… I remember having a sexist teacher in school…but I don't think most teachers don't *intend* to be those things. I like to think most anyway.

This view of racism as existing only in intentional acts is one of the ways that white teachers can fail to address complicity in the institutional forms of racism. By adhering to a view of school standards as culturally neutral, for example, teachers do not acknowledge how those standards act on students of different cultural backgrounds in different and inequitable ways. By creating and using hierarchical categories and where whiteness is at the top, whites actively maintain white privilege and racial inequity. By only acknowledging the intentional forms of racism, whites ignore the hierarchy we have created. So, I tried to use a naming of whiteness with Elizabeth in order to convince her of how I believe that white teachers are complicit in racism when we do not challenge the privilege and dominance we construct and perpetuate.

THE CREATION AND MAINTENANCE OF PRIVILEGE

As we grew more comfortable with each other, Elizabeth and I were able to get into more contentious conversations about what we consider to be instances of racism. I believe it is in these conversations where Elizabeth showed the strongest adherence to liberalism, and she did so specifically in her articulation of behavior standards for students. As I now present her thoughts on these standards, I also show how I tried to challenge her interpretation of them. In addition, I discuss the ways in which Elizabeth (like other white teachers, myself included) potentially bar racial minority students' access to curriculum by uncritically utilizing such standards.

At one point, Elizabeth and I revisited her earlier comments about Latino males, i.e., that their behavior felt aggressive to her. It seemed to me that she had some standards—which she did admit are set by whites according to white cultural norms—that had to apply to all of her students. In our conversations I attempted to challenge Elizabeth on how she used those standards, to get her to see the way in which they created privilege for whites, and to discuss with her the potential effect of that whiteness on her non-white students. My challenge was influenced by the concept of whiteness as property. I attempted to get Elizabeth to admit that by employing these white standards in a way that categorized students according to un-critiqued notions of "good student," she at times might have negatively affected some of her students' access to equal educational opportunities. It is interesting how she responded to my inquiry. When she described how she decided which standards she used, the language she used often marked what she claimed were white standards as the "highest" standards. She also tried to challenge that hierarchy once it was pointed out to her.

> Ben: [Referring back to our discussion about interpreting Latino male student behavior as aggressive:] I guess I'm trying to see where interpretation becomes judgment.
>
> Elizabeth: Ahh!
>
> Ben: It's complicated… Interpretations seem to me to have consequences.

Elizabeth: Yes.

Ben: Like when we interpret something as aggressive… sometimes aggressive is considered okay. It's *rarely* considered okay in that type of situation in school. So if we categorize something like that [the behavior of her Latino male students] as aggressive, then does that not potentially have negative consequences on people?

Here was an early attempt by me to utilize the concept of whiteness as property. By categorizing certain types of behavior as aggressive, I believe teachers can unintentionally use a standard of whiteness to exclude certain people from the privileges of that whiteness. For example, Elizabeth could potentially use the label of aggressive to categorize her Latino students as students who do not exhibit the appropriate cultural norms. In essence, they would be categorized as non-white. A potential consequence of this practice is that these students could have a more limited access to—in effect, they could actually be excluded from—the same classroom experience as students who are categorized more in more positive ways. Even if they have some access to similar curriculum and instruction (e.g., they are in the same classes as the rest of the students), they may not have it in equitable ways. Because these students do not have the right to use and enjoy the privileges that whiteness offers them, teachers may discipline and teach students categorized in such ways differently from students who have privilege. As our conversation continues, Elizabeth shows how categorization can begin to affect students' access to privilege.

Elizabeth: I completely agree with you [referring to how the label of aggressive can lead to negative consequences]. There's a problem with what you said.

Ben: Okay. Good.

Elizabeth: You said "in school." Cultural norms unfortunately play such a profound role in how we make rules that there has to be some bottom line, and that might come from any number of places. So, we have a bottom line, which is that you will not sexually harass people, and the definition of what sexual harassment was came from the culture making the rules, and so in our culture it is inappropriate to walk up to a woman and put your arm between her legs [which one of her Latino male students did]. It was [inappropriate] in their culture, too, apparently…

Ben: And realizing that he was the exception… [She acknowledged this earlier.]

Elizabeth: Yeah, he was. But he had a pack with him. Middle schoolers run in these packs and he was the front man for this pack thing. And nobody else was doing that, but they were sort of supporting him in that role. So, in a school, that was over the top. And one of the reasons—and I think when you're [the teacher] making rules, you've got to set the bar kind of up here [indicated high with her hand] because when you've got three very disparate cultures coming together, all of them with strong backing and strong tradition on their side, you have to have a much higher standard. Like you have to go with the highest.

Elizabeth's comments illustrate two of the practices by which some white teachers use whiteness [i.e., a view that white cultural norms are more appropriate than other cultural norms] to assign or restrict students' access to the privileges that come with whiteness. The first practice was that of constructing, employing, and reinforcing a racialized category of appropriate behavior. I noticed that "up here" to Elizabeth indicated that the white standard was highest (and shortly I will show how I challenged her on this). It seemed that Elizabeth saw the white standard of behavior as the one that all students should follow because it she thought it was the most strict. So, this first practice—using a hierarchy of standards with those based on white ways of being at the top—contributed to the second practice—namely, the attribution of one non-white person's behavior to an entire group. Observing one Latino boy sexually harass a girl was not separated from what Elizabeth thought was aggressive behavior on the part of the Latino boys as a group. So, even though the rest of the boys did not harass the girl, Elizabeth's comments indicated that they were still complicit in the inappropriate act – "they were sort of supporting him in that role." Latino boys in this case were categorized as group of students who did not live up to the acceptable standards of the school because of the actions of one boy. They were also denied the white privilege of having individual actions being attributed to the entire group. Thus, Elizabeth created and then employed a hierarchy where white behavior was seen as the most appropriate for school, and then she used that hierarchy to interpret the behavior of her Latino male students in a way that denied them privilege and equitable treatment.

I was able to challenge the way in which Elizabeth denied her Latino students access to the privileges of whiteness and the way in which she viewed standards of behavior along a racial hierarchy. As our conversation continued, we talked about how different racial groups can have different standards of what is considered appropriate and I tried to challenge how she viewed those differences in potentially marginalizing ways. For example, Elizabeth talked about the difference in what cultural groups consider to be appropriate personal space. As Elizabeth pointed out the different preferences of her students, I asked her about how she positions those differences in a hierarchy of appropriateness.

Ben: What is the highest standard in that circumstance?

Elizabeth: The most *uptight* standard is the white people…

Ben: And that's the highest standard?

Elizabeth: Okay, so…

Ben: You did say highest before [when talking about which standard you have to apply in classrooms with a mix of racial groups].

Elizabeth: I mean highest setting the bar the highest. Not the highest in the sense of the moral point of view. Highest in terms of the highest…

Ben: I'm trying to understand what you mean.

Elizabeth: What I was thinking was… Oh, I guess highest is often used as sort of an exceptional thing. No, what I was meaning was that it's got the most rules applied to it. Like the most criteria… So you said in school… but then *outside* of school and between people who are old enough that know what they are doing… So, what I consider appropriate in school has got to be a different standard for me. Like I joke with my friends, "Oh, I'm being Ms. Corporate now." And that's because I'm suddenly this completely uptight must-have-this-many-rules person as opposed to how adults in society and the world can interact.

I still question her method for determining which standards she applied—e.g., was having the most rules applied to a standard also the most *equitable* way to set that standard, what were the potential consequences of setting the "most rules," and did these standards affect different groups of students in different ways? It still seemed that by merely using the "most rules" was still working from an understanding that rules are culturally neutral, that all rules affect all students in the same way. I was trying to get Elizabeth to consider the language she uses in explaining her rule making process. In our interviews at least, she also had to articulate that process and not take it for granted. In fact, while I do not think I moved Elizabeth's thinking on standards as much as I would have liked during the course of our interviews, my questioning of her thinking did often force her into such articulations, and there were times where Elizabeth did admit that she had to think about her opinions and practices more. In these areas, I saw the potential for challenging the remnants of liberal ideology in her practice.

I use the word remnants because it was in those situations where I felt Elizabeth shifted in and out of an adherence to liberal forms of racial understanding. Hers was not an absolute belief in the neutrality of standards. Often, as I believe several of the excerpts above show, she resigned herself to universal standards because she saw no other recourse in practice. Her thoughts on complicity were contradictory, at times not seeing that there were more things teachers could do to challenge complicity even though at other times her comments made it sound that when actually teaching, she did in fact look for ways to do more. One possible factor that may have limited her ability to see new possibilities was the way in which she viewed the role and status of teachers as actors in the structure of schooling. With regard to racism, she certainly acknowledged that the structure of schooling has a racist dynamic to it and that blacks and Latinos suffer most from that dynamic. However, she had a harder time seeing how teachers promote that cycle of racism. Even though my above challenges to her categorizing practices did not get her to question those practices as much as I would have liked, our sustained dialogue on the racialized construction of standards got us to a place where she began to question her beliefs on complicity a bit more.

The following interaction shows Elizabeth struggling to understand how this complicity exists. Specifically, she struggled with the idea of intention in relation to complicity in racial disparity.

> Ben: It sounds like your talking about racism as an intentional act. [She smiles, and then there is a long pause.] I'm not saying that's bad or good, I'm just trying to get at what you think.
>
> Elizabeth: I didn't smile because I thought you were wrong [at my interpretation of her definition]; I smiled because I realized I'm not sure.
>
> Ben: So if I say, "there is racism," what does that mean?
>
> Elizabeth: Well what I was going to say—before you said "intentional"—[then there is a long pause as she is thinking of how to word this]...racism is *judging* based on racist stereotypes...and assuming superiority based on that judgment. Is that highfalutin?
>
> Ben: So, judging based on stereotypes and...
>
> Elizabeth: Assuming superiority... Now the intentional part of that... [pause] ... I've actually wondered this before and I have talked to people before. We did a day-long seminar on difference, and one of my teammates who is black came out of her room afterwards and—and she's a very good friend of mine, we're family—what she was saying to me was that during that seminar, it [racism] had been defined as judging people on what I had just said, but I guess to me ... so I come to this with preconceived ideas. I can't help it. I grew up in a world that hands me these ideas. I think to me racism is when you ignore the truth that your presented... I don't know how to put this that's making sense...

As I tried to nail down her thoughts on intent, Elizabeth made comments like those above in which her own articulation of intent shifted. In other words, it was unclear to me whether she meant that in order to name a practice as racist, whites had to simply not see new truths or we had to intentionally ignore those new truths once we saw them, and this was an important distinction for me. The belief that if whites unwittingly ignore "new truths" they are not responsible for perpetuating racism seems to be one I can critique, and thus it is an opening to promote more critical understandings of racism through dialogue. I wanted Elizabeth to acknowledge that both forms of unawareness—intentional or unintentional—could have the same negative consequences, so I questioned her on this.

> Ben: So, intentionally ignore or...?

> Elizabeth: But that's now where I'm having trouble. I think intentionally.
>
> Ben: So you just don't know…
>
> Elizabeth: If I have an idea… If I have a racial idea and I'm right because a lot of people have told me this or it's been implied repeatedly by society and then I bang into a situation that proves that stereotype wrong, if I continue to believe it because it makes me feel better about myself, *that's* racism. However, we don't always *plan* to do that, so that's where I'm still having trouble with that word "intentional," like we might not realize that we…like we like to think that we're…I know I'm not answering your question—it's because I really don't know. I think human beings are very, very capable of self-justifying—like, "My behavior is okay because…" and we don't consciously necessarily go through that process. It's just there. Like, "It will mess up my little world if I have to admit that that is not true.

This excerpt points to the value of digging into whites' understanding of racism and complicity. I was able to get Elizabeth to think about her beliefs about how intent relates to complicity. I believe getting teachers like Elizabeth to focus on the language they use is important. Drawing from Hall (1997), Madison (2005) states, "Representation has consequences: How people are represented is how they are treated" (p. 4). So, how people represent other people affects how they will treat those other people. The language that teachers use to describe students, then, enables them to solidify and legitimate (or as Elizabeth said, to self-justify) the way they treat their students. As teachers can use language to sanction the way they categorize or apply standards, interrogating this language is a step towards affecting those modes of categorization. To again paraphrase Delgado and Stefancic (2000), the modes of categorization that people employ influence the way they dominate others, thus understanding these modes can lead to dismantling their oppressive nature. As Langellier and Patterson (2004) argue, brining how people perform their discourses (such as on race) to the fore can affect how they act based on those discourses.

I believe that I could have perhaps pushed Elizabeth to draw on more critical understandings of racism when discussing teachers' complicity had a connected the part of our conversation where we discuss the issue of intentionality in racism back to the parts where we discussed the standards that she used with her students. In our discussions on intent, Elizabeth was able to question and think about the interplay between teachers' actions and societal structures that marginalize students of color in a somewhat open way. She resisted this relationship more when she discussed the standards she used to label students. Perhaps by bringing the issue of standards back into our dialogue on how intent is or is not an aspect of racism we might have been able to find more common ground on how teachers' use of standards in racialized ways leads to complicity in institutional racism. It would have brought the language of whiteness as property and systems of categorization back in a potentially fruitful way, one in which we would have been better able to jointly analyze the shortcomings of liberal interpretation of racism in order to better understand the issue of complicity.

DIVERSIONS, ACKNOWLEDGEMENTS, AND LEARNING

Elizabeth's acknowledgements of complicity rarely came without a "yes, but...". In other words, even when she agreed with my articulation of the racial dynamic of school practice, she also had to challenge at least some part of that articulation. These challenges usually occurred by diverting from my questions and examples and then by using her own examples. Her examples often used what I deemed to be extreme language (as I will show below) and hypothetical situations (though I believe they were at times based on real ones). These diversions had the effect of keeping me on my toes. They taught me how to more deeply analyze the racial understandings of a white person who still relied on aspects of liberal ideology to explain racial disparity—especially in the sense that school practices were culturally neutral and thus did not contribute to that disparity—and I had to constantly think of new ways to respond to that logic. They also highlighted both the effective and ineffective ways I articulated complicity.

For example, Elizabeth especially disliked solutions to racism that threatened a liberal sense of meritocracy. In the following interaction I ask Elizabeth if minority students were faced with and affected by racism in ways that white students were not. This is a clear and typical example of her "yes, but..." type of response.

> Elizabeth: Okay, I think the simple answer is, yes. I think that everybody deals with racism, but there are more problems for anybody who is a minority student.
>
> Ben: Okay, so then if you have minority students, do you think it is... how do you think teachers should respond? Is it the teacher's responsibility to then to do things that they might not do for white students?
>
> Elizabeth: No. [She says this very quickly.] Wait, wait... uh okay... It's kind of like my problem with affirmative action. I understand it's one of the better ways to get kids into colleges. Absolutely we have to get minority kids into colleges, absolutely. And we have that background and we're never going to break the cycle on stuff... but I don't think it's good for anybody if I simply say, "Oh no, I know you didn't understand this because of who you are, so I'll just ignore that answer on that test."

I find it interesting that Elizabeth immediately equated doing special things for minority students with dumbing down the curriculum or low standards. When asked if minority students face challenges white students do not, Elizabeth agreed but also calls it the "simple" answer. So, one part of Elizabeth's response is that she did not want to simply agree with my assertion about racism. I believe another part of her response clung to a liberal notion of universalism, of the universal subject, a notion that is based on a view of society and its institutions being culturally neutral. What is good or bad for one person is good or bad for everybody regardless of racial background. A teacher cannot make exceptions because of a person's race because that would imply that they have to go out of their way for any individual because of specific circumstances. This type of response upholds the idea that "we" (all people regardless of race, gender, cultural background, etc.) are all inherently the same. This type of thinking does not recognize that the view of the universal subject is based on a white ideal. So, it is of course impossible to think of a remedy to inequity that centers on race as such a remedy challenges the notion of inherent sameness. Therefore, racial disparity is caused by intentional acts of racism or by the victims of that disparity. It becomes the responsibility of these victims to overcome it even if they do face challenges that that those with racial privilege do not.

In addition, Elizabeth saw minority students as facing specific challenges related to race but did not always see it as the teacher's responsibility to counteract that fact, and I of course wanted to challenge the latter notion. So, I was trying to get Elizabeth to think of things that teachers could do to help minority students succeed, and interestingly enough, I believe Elizabeth did some of this in her teaching practice. However, she did not put this aspect of her practice in racial terms. This might be because she would do it for any student who had a particular issue to face that got in the way if his or her learning; and while this was probably true, I also believe that acknowledging a student's background relies on a racial awareness, one in which I believe Elizabeth actually had. Elizabeth's adherence to a colorblind ideology actually prevented her from seeing her own practice in racial terms. In addition, while I believe she practiced aspects of a racially conscious pedagogy, I also believe it is important to challenge teachers like Elizabeth on the liberal, colorblind remnants of their thinking. As I stated before, the language people use has consequences.

In Elizabeth's case, my hope was that I could get her to expand her racial consciousness generally and to revision practices such as affirmative action more specifically. Without getting into a discussion about the various types of affirmative action and what they actually do,[2] in this case what I think is important for white teachers to understand is that policies that pay attention to race (i.e., use race as a central construct in decision-making) do not inherently promote lower standards. So, I challenged Elizabeth on her articulation of affirmative action, which she implied meant lower standards for minority students.

> Ben: [Referring to her comment in the previous excerpt:] Do you think that's what Affirmative Action does?
>
> Elizabeth: No, but I think that that's one of the problems is that people don't understand how to address [racial disparity], and so they think making the exception is like that… So, okay… [laughs because of the delicacy of the conversation]… I'm going to say no I don't do anything special, but then…I'm what you call a demanding teacher, so I tend to find myself trying to get kids to come in for extra help a lot… and, most of the people I find I try to come in are boys [hesitation in her voice]… and more… I don't

> know… and people from minority groups… just because they're not doing as well. So is that doing something special? No, because I would do it for anybody. But then I go to the kids that are struggling in my class and encourage them to come for extra help, and coincidentally they're black.
>
> Ben: Do you think it's coincidental?
>
> Elizabeth: No, because I think that I teach in a certain style that is really demanding and very highbrow, big words and stuff, and I think that the language I use is a language that you're only going to be exposed to if you live in households with parents who understand what "didactic" means, for example. So, I think that I am a victim of my own upbringing enough to... I have to teach from where I am.

Here, she recognized that there was some racial aspect of how she spoke and taught and that this could have an affect on her students' access to the curriculum. The conversation continued:

> Ben: So then you wouldn't go out of your way to change your language…?
>
> Elizabeth: Well, I was actually going to say something else which is that we did this weird thing at Cardinal [her previous school] which was that we studied this what-kind-of-learner-are-you test, you know are you kinetic, auditory, or whatever, and a much larger percentage of our black kids were auditory learners. So, I am a very auditory teacher, so on some level what I'm actually doing should appeal more to…but then the language I'm using… and yes, to answer I do every once in a while—quite often—try to put it in their language or like explain it or sum it up and then they laugh at me because I'm trying to speak their language, but then maybe they get it which is the main point. Wow! That's a disaster! I don't know. [We both laugh.] I don't know if I addressed the issues or not.

Elizabeth to some extent did recognize that going out of her way to make sure students understood meant breaking down her paradigm of teaching and her discourse style (not to mention her views on standards) to some degree. She acknowledged the racial and class aspects of her speech and general discourse style and could even imagine how her style may have worked well with her primarily African American students. To some degree, this was the way in which Elizabeth broke from liberal thought. Rather than only alter her teaching in ways that fit within her current way of speaking, she knew that changing her speech might help students, so she was willing to do that. So when I posed a very simple challenge to her comment, "I have to teach where I am," Elizabeth could envision potential adaptations to her speech that provided challenges, even if only simple ones, to liberal notions of universal and colorblind pedagogy. Her last comment, "what a disaster!" referred to the messiness of her response to my questioning, indicating to me that by delving more deeply into her thoughts on the dynamic of race allowed for potential self-analysis of her thinking.

To me the messiness indicated that she was trying to think through the racialized facets of her thought and practice. Importantly, following up with her diversions, sticking with them in our conversation, allowed us to come to some acknowledgement of the racial aspects of action. At the same time, I had not yet developed a language that helped lead to that acknowledgement early in our dialogue. I believe the interviews with Elizabeth did eventually help with such a language, but it was not until near the end of our conversations that I began to envision how to promote awareness in racial terms without also instilling in white teachers a sense of being personally blamed. Later in the chapter, I will describe more how the interviews with Elizabeth were educative to me.

So, despite the instances of where Elizabeth could revision her practice in racial terms, my method of interviewing did not sustain such revisionism. She would often go back to comments that indicated that her thinking still retained many other pretenses of liberal ideology. It was still hard for her to imagine changes that did not fit within the current structure of schooling. For example, observe the following interaction.

> Ben: ...probably most students can succeed in higher-level classes.
>
> Elizabeth: They can't, and not because of racism.
>
> Ben: And that's where I disagree. I think most students can succeed in higher- level classes.
>
> Elizabeth: Sure, if there's ten people in the class and I can spend two hours working with you personally because you don't know any of the background whereas the kid sitting next to you knew it all already and I could...

Here she was critiquing the structure of traditional middle school classrooms. She had a good point that that structure does affect a teacher's ability to promote equitable pedagogy. However, given that structure is what it currently is, she again could not imagine what teachers could do to work against racial disparity. She could not see a solution to the disparity. So, she diverted the responsibility for it to the "system," to use Stephanie's word from chapter 2, and away from teachers. I did not help as I countered her statements without offering her information to back up my claims.

Part of the motivation for Elizabeth to divert away teachers' responsibility was probably due to the teachers she worked with—"I understand that I actually am a little privileged. I've worked with *amazing* teachers at both schools..."—and to the fact that some of her comments about the disabling aspect of the structure of schooling may have been accurate.

> Elizabeth: At Cardinal, a school of 1,200 students, it was much more the rules were the rules. It was a lot of students. The rule had to be much more the rule because it was just that big, and because assistant principals had stacks of discipline forms on their desk, and you can't take this amazing amount of time. But then at Phoenix with 190 students, and this is a big year,

> like the way my teammate and I do discipline is when two kids are in a fight, we pull them out separately and we talk to them separately, and then we bring them together and then there is the result of that. And there was a discipline thing on Friday and it took us—I was supposed to be coaching a soccer game and the other coach had to do it all alone because for about an hour I was working with my teammate. The two of us were working to resolve a problem between two kids. You just don't have the amount of time to do that in a traditional public school.

So, I do agree with Elizabeth that racially aware practice can be made much harder depending on the structure of a school. However, what is also interesting to me here is that she chose to work at Phoenix. She recognized that she could construct more equitable responses to students because of being at a smaller, more community-focused school. As much as Elizabeth challenged that there was anything more teachers could do, by pushing her to continue to think about the accuracy of that thought, I was able to get Elizabeth to see how she challenged her own statements, if only in the context of a small, community-based school. Perhaps if I had followed up on her decision to teach at Phoenix or if I had delved into her practices at both Phoenix and Cardinal, I might have been able to get Elizabeth develop language that put her practice into racial terms and perhaps see more possibility for teachers in working towards racial equity. Likewise, perhaps if I had examined with Elizabeth the positive ways she did practice antiracist pedagogy, I would have been better able to develop language that can more effectively communicate with white teachers about our complicity and how to challenge it.

COMPLICTY, BLAME, AND THE PEDAGOGICAL

We kept going back and forth about teachers' responsibility and the potential for change within the current structure of schooling. A key pedagogical aspect of this dialogue was our discussion on the meaning and use of the word "racist." This part of our discussion helped me learn how to respond to diversions from teachers' responsibility in the construction of critically antiracist responses. I learned to think more about how certain uses of the word "racism" could label white teachers, and I learned a little more about how to name whiteness and draw out complicity in racism without resorting to such labeling. In fact, much of the following interaction helped me think through a book chapter I had written about that subject.[3] In addition, and very importantly, it is during this part of our conversation where a real opening in the liberalism of Elizabeth's thought seemed to occur. In many ways this was the most dialogic part of our interviews. She was still challenging, I was still challenging back, but we were also both receptive to each other's arguments, so the conversation was more immediately pedagogical for both of us.

It was using the language of property analysis (i.e., access to curriculum) that helped me learn how to articulate complicity without assigning blame.

> Ben: Why do you think [the word "racism" is] pejorative?

> Elizabeth: I think because I associate it so closely with the word racist. And because I think...
>
> Ben: But why is racist a pejorative word?
>
> Elizabeth: Because... racist behavior is not just differentiating differences between the races. It's, in my opinion, it is using those differences to subjugate, to downplay another's racial aspect.
>
> Ben: Do you see it therefore as somehow intentional?
>
> Elizabeth: Not necessarily.
>
> Ben: Okay. So, you think even though there's this pejorative meaning and that it's a nasty thing... I am trying to get at the intentionality. Some people see racist like it's I do certain things as a teacher that prevent some of my minority students from being able to [access] the conversation as well as the white students, access the material as easily, and that's my discourse style, and I don't notice that and I don't do anything about it, and my discourse prevents some of my minority students from accessing the curriculum as well... If I don't know that I do it, and it happens but I don't know why it happens because nobody tells me. In my view, it doesn't mean that the person is intentionally racist. It doesn't mean that they have prejudice, but it does mean that there are racist outcomes. I'm not labeling the teacher as racist but I'm labeling the outcome as racist. So there's some practice that you're taking part of that leads to racist outcomes.

Here was one of those instances when I really try to nail down how white teachers like myself can be unintentionally complicit in institutional racism. I am learning how to continue to use the word racism but also not reify teachers as racist individuals. To borrow concepts from Buddhist thinking, I did not want to construct any essential sense of racist self—of whites as essentially and a-contextually racist—as such a sense of self leaves no room for change.[4] At the same time, I also thought it was important not to shy away from the terminology of racism and to name it as such since the word denotes the vicious outcomes for those who suffer from it. Though in the previous excerpt I do not believe I did a good job of describing education in terms of property, it was an attempt at property analysis. The language of property analysis—about access to materials, curriculum, and an equal education—helped me put words to the "system" in a way that allowed me to describe it as continually constructed. In addition, this language helped me balance out an acknowledgement that there are actors in racism with an avoidance of the reification of whites as inherently racist individuals. In essence, I was learning how to move from liberal understandings of racism to critical interpretations of antiracism.

As our conversation from above continued, I tried to refine my understanding and articulation of this balance of acknowledgement and blame. This attempt led to an important realization on Elizabeth's part (and here I return to the except I opened the chapter with).

> Elizabeth: Okay… now do you want me to say if I agree with that or not?
>
> Ben: Well, at least tell me what you think about it.
>
> [Pause]
>
> When I'm talking about racist, that's how I'm thinking about racism… When I talk about racism exists and racism as inherent, that doesn't mean that I think most white people hate black people, but I think ways society has been structured… whites have been dominant for a long, long time in society that those things happen that lead to racial inequality. [Through this description often nods and says, "right, right," in affirmation.]
>
> Elizabeth: So do I feel like that's a racist outcome?
>
> Ben: Just tell me what you think about it.
>
> Elizabeth: No I'm still thinking about it…[we both laugh]… Um… I think that that's a position…[still thinking]… I'll say yes keeping in mind that for me racism, racist is always more about the perpetrator than about the results
>
> Ben: So you do have somewhere in there that the word racism always has some derogatory [connotation that people are intentionally prejudiced]…
>
> Elizabeth: I'm afraid I really do, yeah.
>
> Ben: I'm guessing most people do.
>
> Elizabeth: But I just realized I did [laughs].

This was a real "aha" moment in our dialogue. I sensed a substantial shift in Elizabeth's tone after this. It started her to question less in a challenging way and more to understand what teachers can do to fight racism. She was still skeptical about how teachers could possibly combat the institutional structures that promoted racism and she still diverted responsibility from teachers (and even towards minority students themselves at times), but her tone indicated to me that her challenges were, in part, inquiries into what counted as racist behavior (on the part of teachers) and what could be done to change practice.

> Ben: And I would say that, personally for me, when I think about the term and I'm saying that I want to fight racism, including racism by whites and my own racism, I'm not looking at it as labeling myself as a racist person. But some of my actions might be because they lead to racist outcomes. And that

doesn't mean that I want to do it, but to me it's like well, if I can learn how that happens, then I can also change it.

Elizabeth: Well, then, okay... what is it then, seriously, what is it then when... when the student, and I guess in this case the majority student,[5] chooses to not ever come for help, chooses to not to do the homework ever, chooses to write notes to their friend in class? I'm just really trying to understand.

From the struggling in Elizabeth's tone, I think she really was trying to understand, and I believe this shift to wanting to understand occurred in part because of my reiteration to her that I was trying to avoid labeling white teachers. Again, this interaction was very educative for me, as it led me to think more deeply about how to articulate the balance between naming and blaming. It also impelled me to think about what I consider to be racism. In other words, I had to contemplate the more particular details of teacher behavior to see how they might be acts of complicity (in racism as well as other form of subjugation) and then explain that I did not think teachers intentionally wanted to oppress students of color. For example, here is my response to Elizabeth's previous question.

Ben: [What I am trying to say] is that it is on the onus of the teacher to try to figure out what is going on and to try to do something about it.

Elizabeth: And when we try? And we really do change our behavior and our speech patterns and our approach and they still flunk, is it still a racist outcome? [Good question!]

Ben: It *might* be a racist outcome. It doesn't mean that the teacher... I'm not... personally I try to shy away from people as racist because I don't think that most people who go into teaching want that.

So, in our discussion I continued to try and balance an adherence to the word "racism" and an avoidance of assigning blame. Yet despite my attempt to distinguish between complicit and intentional racism, Elizabeth was hesitant to accept the usefulness of my distinction. We continued to bat around these ideas: the word "racism," the idea of complicity, and the locus of the cause for racial disparity. As Elizabeth was very good at coming up with examples (sometimes extreme examples) that challenged my articulation of these issues, our conversation got quite detailed about what purpose such an articulation serves.

Elizabeth: Okay... I will agree with your argument. I'll also say I think it's an incredibly dangerous argument.

Ben: Okay, because?

Elizabeth: Because inherently every single person's behavior therefore can be labeled racist, sexist, ageist, [I insert, "I would agree with that."] and I think it's impossible for us to wander through life having decided that and not assign any blame.

Ben: Here's the two things that I—and I would agree that maybe… I mean part of the process for me is learning how to communicate this without it leading to blame [I briefly mention the Buddhist perspective and the book chapter I wrote]… I am trying to learn how to communicate this in a way that doesn't assign blame. Because that's why I really am careful how I use the words racist and sexist and classist. And that's why I am very clear about my definition meaning about the outcomes and not the intention because I am trying to get away from it being a blame thing. Because once you blame somebody and you label them, and I do this, I just retreat and find a defense as opposed to really addressing what might be the real issue. And that's why sometimes I wonder if racial is better than racist.[6] Is there a racial component…

Elizabeth: I think for most people it's the same.

Ben: …maybe [hesitantly]… but to me saying there's a racial component and there's a racist outcome has a different tone at least. But getting back to your point about everything can be racist, sexist, ageist. I would say, yeah it probably can be. I would agree and maybe it is. My point is I don't think, and this is where you may disagree, I don't think as a white male I can ever completely get away from some of the things I do having racist or sexist outcomes. [Note I include sexist because it may be more of what Elizabeth thinks about as a labels herself a feminist.]

Elizabeth: Intentions or outcomes?

Ben: Outcomes, not intentions.

For me, the idea that whites can never escape racism did not indicate that whites cannot also counter racism, but for Elizabeth it did. In my thinking, revisioning how whites are complicit (via a naming of whiteness) actually creates space for change. Our whiteness may be baggage that hinders our socially just motives but it is not an unmovable weight. It does not prevent us from any movement.

For Elizabeth, on the other hand, whiteness and complicity articulated in such a way was more limiting. It made her divert responsibility for racist and sexist outcomes again to those who suffer from discrimination.

Elizabeth: I think there's no way of getting away from it being racist or sexist outcomes because you're not just dealing in a vacuum, you're dealing with me, my response is going to based on my own…

[And later in the interview…]

> If you were talking to me, as a male talking to a female, you might be working your darnedest to not be sexist, but it might end up that I feel discriminated against or that I feel or whatever, even if you were working your best. But that's *my* response. You might have actually done everything right. Well, by whatever definition of right there is. This is my point. If you're not working in a vacuum, *my* response is also going to be conditioned by my own experience. So, you might have absolutely let me have my say and whatever you need to do, but because you didn't respond to one question I asked, and I've had conditioning that makes me feel that that means a man is ignoring me. So, I guess my problem with labeling...I'd say it was a two-way thing. And so I think it becomes... therefore I think it's dangerous. Does that make sense?

Elizabeth thought about those cases where whites have done "everything right" and minorities still feel as if racism is present. While I do not doubt that such examples may exist—or at least may potentially exist—I do not feel as if they are representative of the way whites interact most of the time, nor do I find such extreme examples useful for counteracting racism. At the time of the interview I did find Elizabeth's comments very interesting because they made me think of why I find it so necessary to focus on the responsibility of, to use Elizabeth's word, the "perpetrators" of racism. I also think it is important that Elizabeth included the phrase, "Well, by whatever definition of right there is." This indicated an acknowledgement on her part of the social construction of right and wrongs and indicated an opening into how to question her about how whites are dominant in those constructions. These are the places where I think whites can be questioned about how we categorize in ways that maintain our own privilege and contribute to structural forms of racism.

> Ben: Okay. I'd agree it's a two-way thing, but I guess it's—and I think it's a very interesting way to look at it. I am going to have to think about this more [she laughs and I admit that she makes a good point]. But what I think is that... when racism... even when a black person's, a black student's response, even if it was not intentioned by a white teacher in a racial way and they did things to fight against that racist quality, and a black person still gets some kind racial negative connotation from it, that is still in my opinion—I agree they [the black students] have some play there, they have some action—to me they are still the victim of the racism. They are still the one being materially affected. So, I still think it—I guess what I would say is that I agree with you, but if my intention really is to be good, don't blame them either, and don't blame myself. Don't blame them and say, "Well I tried and they're really not trying," which may be the case, but to think of it that way, to always keep thinking about, well how can I [the teacher] still be compassionate.

This last point was key to me—my own "aha" moment—and it was Elizabeth's questioning that made me realize how essential it was to how I have thought about racism. Through these intense and open discussions I realized that my articulation about white's complicity in racism was about accepting responsibility. It was, and is, about whites accepting responsibility for their part in racial disparity no matter what other factors may be involved and accepting the responsibility to try and do something to challenge racism regardless of those other factors. It is not to ignore those factors but to work against racism even when realizing all the factors that contribute to it. So, critical antiracism involves countering racism regardless of whether or not whites are intentionally responsible for racial disparity. As I said, this was a real "aha" moment for me. At the time of the interview I was not yet able to explain my ideas on responsibility. Reflecting back on the conversation, however, has helped me put words to my agenda as a teacher educator attempting to adhere to a social justice approach to education. Looking back over my interviews with Elizabeth (as well as with the other teachers), I realized that there were several areas in our interviews where I attempted to explain this type of responsibility, but it was Elizabeth's challenging that helped me see and articulate critical antiracism more clearly.

Power is an additional issue that is important in understanding responsibility, and it was a largely unexamined factor in our discussion. Elizabeth gave the example of someone (a hypothetical person) trying to do "everything right," or everything they could to not take part in oppressive behavior. She also, however, alluded to the fact that varying definitions of right and wrong could exist. Through my discussion with Elizabeth I realized that I believe it is the responsibility of those with power (especially those in positions like teachers) to be reflexive about the ways they define right and wrong if they are going to support equitable approaches to education. As whites maintain privilege and power through our systems of categorization, white educators must recognize our part in the reification of our power via such systems. In addition, as those who have suffered from discrimination have an understanding of it that those with power do not (Matsuda, 1995/1987; Delpit, 1995), it is the responsibility of those of us with power who desire to be socially just educators to draw from the wisdom of those who suffer from discrimination in order to understand our privilege, power, and complicity.

CONCLUSION

As I have reiterated many times in this study, I believe a dialogic approach to challenging whites on their complicity is important. Researchers can employ dialogue that carefully balances a maintenance of their epistemological motivations with a respectful acknowledgement of the experiences and social constructions that influence their co-performers in the research in order to motivate whites to question the construction of our systems of categorization, privilege, and worldview. Such a balance can still push whites to think differently while also avoiding labeling whites as racists. It can avoid assigning blame in an unproductive way and can instead promote more reflection on the part of whites, at least of those who want to combat racial disparity.

During my conversations with Elizabeth, I came to a deeper understanding of what it meant to promote such open dialogue—i.e., to be dialogic. I understood better what it meant to be coming from different viewpoints. From earlier interviews with other teachers and from conversations with my pre-service teachers, I knew that I often had a different understanding of complicity from many other white educators. However, from the interviews with Elizabeth, I began to understand how these different understandings could be put into dialogue in order to make new meaning and come to understandings that potentially support an antiracist practice. We were able to shift from discussing the accuracy of CRT to white teachers' complicity in racism and then to teacher's responsibility to counteract racism. While I do not believe we got into the specifics about what teachers can do as much as either of us would have liked, I do believe we both put teacher responsibility into question.

We each drew on our own experiences to discuss the possibility of what teachers can do. For example, Elizabeth mentioned a student she had in class.

> Elizabeth: I had a student last year... she's definitely a very good in-class student. She never was loud. She never was disruptive. She always did her homework. Even though she obviously hadn't tried much, at least she had tried something, so she was in many ways a perfect in-class student, but I also know she spent a lot of time in class writing notes to her friends. She doesn't really care, and she was absent the day of a test, and she was often absent the days of tests. So, I arranged for her to take it the next day at lunch. She didn't do it. I arranged for her the following day after school. She didn't do it. And I was her soccer coach, and she was supposed to do it the next day, her third attempt, and she came to soccer practice instead, and I said, "No." And she's like, "Well, I'm going to go back now and take it," and I said, "No." And she was just stunned that I cut her off, like I had not done up until that point. And I actually think I had done her a disservice by being so accommodating. She just absolutely expected that when it was convenient for her, which would be never, but when it was convenient for her to take that test, that's when it was going to be available....[After she said no] she was never absent for another day there was a test...

For Elizabeth, deviating from the policy had negative consequences on this student, and when she "cut her off," the student was actually better off. However, I do not think her example showed a strict adherence to her classroom policy. She was able to be strict with her student because she also had a relationship with her. Elizabeth made a decision based on knowing this student individually and not because it was what she would do in every case. I also countered her example with one of my own.

> Ben: It's an interesting case. I guess when I try to look at, even for myself, when I think about how I would address it...I think about a similar student in DC that we had at this charter school. It was hard to get him to do anything. I mean was hard to get him not to swear...we had this policy, swear three times and your out, but if we had held to that, he would have been out in a day...so in his case, he wasn't doing anything, was it better for him to be in school or is it better form him to be out of school?

> …With this guy, if we had kicked him out of school, he would have been gone. But two years later, when I was gone from the school, he actually was getting ready to pass the GED. And I would have never have guessed that he would even have done that. I would never have guessed it. So, for him it wasn't the three-strikes-and-you're-out that helped him. It was that he needed time to acclimate to the… he was a drug addict, he came from no family, all different things… Maybe sometimes it can be too much slack, but in the end if the kid's out of school, what services does the student get? I mean to me I agree that your example is interesting, but what happens next is also a very important part of the issue.

I tried to use this example to show how policies can have consequences that we (educators who honestly care about our students) do not actually want to come about and how working against such policies can be positive. Even when Elizabeth was initially resistant to interpreting my example in the same way that I did, she did also articulate how she would have responded.

> Elizabeth: There's two responses to that… One, I would look at the effect of that behavior on the students in the classroom. Like, what happened to the students around him? If you tell him you're gone if you keep doing this and you continue to disturb everybody's work? And that is… if we are looking at results as opposed to intentions, then we have to look at that result. What happened to other students in the class? What happened to their ability to follow what teachers say seeing that example? Okay, the second thing is what I would have done with that kid, and it's of course so easy for me to say what I would have done because I'm not there and not irritated or trying to help him, I would have suspended him for a day and then re-wrote the policy with him. And I would have said, I would have integrated it more slowly.

So, Elizabeth still focused on this student's behavior and how it did not fit in with a classroom structure (as it existed in ideal form in her mind). I certainly do understand that she worked in a public school, the context of which makes it very difficult to interpret and respond to students as individuals. Despite that context, she was able to think about how she might adjust the school policy to work for this student. In fact, as we discussed earlier, working at a smaller, charter school helped Elizabeth think about these types of solutions.

So, for Elizabeth, constructing solutions to racial disparity entailed thinking about teachers as complicit actors in institutional racism and beginning to resist liberal interpretations of possible challenges to that disparity. She was learning to articulate how she balanced the difficulty of the contexts in which she has worked with how she approached her responsibility to be equitable. For me, putting teacher responsibility into question helped me learn how to more clearly articulate how I think teachers are responsible for racism and how they can counteract their own complicity. A large part of this new articulation meant trying to name (i.e., to name whiteness and complicity without blaming. As I briefly mentioned earlier, I worked this out for myself through a use of Buddhist concepts, an area I have been and will able to continue to explore in my professional life. In addition, I was able to draw on personal examples that helped show what the focusing on teacher responsibility (versus student or parent responsibility) could look like.

Even though we drew from different points of reference, we were both able to see each other's point of view because of the dialogic approach to the conversation. Because we stuck with these stories and dissected them together, we were both able to move in our thinking a bit and come to mutual respect and understanding of where each of us was coming from and how we might be able to think and act in different ways. Small interactions—such as the one above in which we compare our reactions to struggling students—illustrate how we were able to maintain our own positions and *also* incorporate the other's thinking into our own.

I attempted to position Elizabeth as an equal in our dialogue. My sense is that she truly felt as one. At one point when I was concerned that the conversation might seem like I was attacking her too much, she replied, "Are you kidding, I love this stuff!" Elizabeth's willingness to discuss the sticky issue of race enabled me to challenge her on her adherence to liberalism and for her to explain how she actually did resist it at times. Liberalism and colorblindness were really moving targets (not a simple dichotomy of support and challenge). It took a real sticking with it to get at it at all. More than any other interview, this one moved from the focus of understanding what the issues are to more detailed discussion of how teachers can find new ways to think and act. I had learned from Sarah to think of CRT as dialogic performance and this set of interviews with Elizabeth gave me the chance to practice it as such.

In summation, I want to reiterate that it was Elizabeth's motivation to work against racial disparity that helped us both learn from this dialogue. Even though she relied on liberal notions of antiracism at times, she also practices aspects of critical antiracism. Specifically, she challenged the cultural neutrality of curriculum and classroom discourse in order to make her classroom more equitable for her non-white students. Furthermore, her willingness to bring her practice into dialogue with me knowing I would challenge her in some aspects of that practice allowed us both to form new ways to promote more critical antiracist practice. Finally, what I learned from Elizabeth has helped me reconsider and potentially re-narrate the earlier dialogues of this study. With Stephanie, I can now understand her thinking and practice as antiracist in intent. It is her adherence to liberal forms of that antiracism that may prevent her from realizing the racial equity she actually does want to promote. With Melissa and Sarah, I can now see aspects of their practice as already critically antiracist. In retrospect, our dialogue helped us all better understand it as such. Discussions that included an attention to CRT gave us some of the tools to better analyze school experiences so as to better promote the racial equity they are already working towards.

NOTES

1. In fact, a large reason of why she enjoyed being in this study was that I attempted to treat her as an equal and position her as and educational expert.
2. Feagin and O'Brien (2003) provide a concise description of the types of affirmative action and how affirmative action is often "misrepresented by many whites" (p. 194).

[3] Blaisdell, B. (2005). "Sitting with Ourselves: How to Work Against White Guilt in Anti-Racist Teacher Education." In S. Hughes (Ed.), What We Still Don't Know About Race: How to Talk About it in the Classroom. Mellen Press: Lewiston, NY.

[4] Again, I explain these Buddhist concepts and this argument in more detail in the book chapter in mentioned previously.

[5] The majority of students at her school were African American.

[6] Interestingly, in the editing process for my book chapter, the book's editor often changed where I wrote "racist" and inserted "racial." I am still undecided about which word is more accurate and/or more useful.

CHAPTER 5

THE BOYS

Performing Antiracist Narratives

> Yeah, the idea that it's very nice to have a warm place in my heart that I can go back to at all times. And when you see people who don't have that sense of something concrete and solid that you can call your mother and father and get warm feelings to be back on par again, when you see kids who don't have that option, that ability, through other means, you can come to empathize with them at least, and see the gaps, see the holes, see the weakness, and say, "I want to do more for that other person" because no one else is going to do it for them. – Elijah, high school history teacher.

> I think art is also one of those tools that is incredibly educational to see the better side and to experience true creativity and expression of humanity. I think there's just something magical that lives in the ability to open your spirit up to art, poetry, you know and see with poetic eyes. When you see with poetic eyes you look at the beauty and the hope and the potential of humanity and not just the history and way it is and how it's securing your privileged state. – John, high school English teacher.

The two voices above show the tenor of the dialogue I had with the three male high school teachers who I call "The Boys." When I first used this moniker (in my notes and in conversations with a colleague), I used it somewhat jokingly. These were three men who all worked as at the same high school, who I knew before the study—though only one well—and who thought it would be good to do the interviews all together. So, for most of the interviews, we spoke outside around a table, food grilling in the background, and in the first interview I immediately got the sense that this conversation was different from the others. For one, the casual atmosphere made it hard for me to dive right into interviewing in the same direct way I did with the women in the study. It was almost as if we had to speak as friends first. Two, we were all men. I did not know why and how that changed the way I worked with these teachers at first, but I do believe there are differences in how I question and challenge men and women on their beliefs. Later in this chapter I will draw from Gilligan's (1982) work (along with a critique of that work) to discuss differences in how men and women relate to caring with the hope to describe, in part, how I interacted differently with these teachers. Three, I quickly realized that the two these teachers quoted above—Elijah and John—relatively young men in their late twenties, had very in-depth understandings about the racial dynamics that exist in schools and society. They had thought about it a lot, and they articulated their approach to racial equity according to critical interpretations of antiracism. Furthermore, they use these critical understandings as primary motivations for their teaching. So, the way I positioned myself in relation to these teachers very much changed as compared to the other teachers I interviewed. A couple of the other teachers from previous chapters were also very astute about social justice issues. Sarah and Melissa both had a strong racial awareness but positioned themselves as learners with me. Elizabeth had a strong social justice motivation but was hesitant to put her practice into racial terms and examine it that way. Elijah and John, on the other hand, had a strong racial consciousness, put their practice into racial terms, and articulated racial equity as a prime motivation for their teaching. They understood teaching and education from a racial perspective. This is not to say that the women did not work towards racial equity in equally substantive or effective ways or that The Boys were better at realizing racial equity but rather that the articulations these two men in particular corresponded more closely with my own articulation of antiracist practice.

These above factors, in essence, made this set of interviews much more of a discussion about how white educators can articulate an intentionally antiracist pedagogy and how these white men came to believe in such an approach. In our conversations we performed ourselves—or at least aspects of ourselves—as socially just, antiracist educators. It often felt as if we were very much four colleagues batting around ideas over food and drink on summer nights. So, I use the title, The Boys, more now to emphasize the playful (though still deep) tenor of our dialogue and to keep the emphasis that we were talking as a group and to highlight the difference in how I conducted the interviews.

Because of this different focus, CRT actually had less of a direct impact on how I interpreted the dialogue, and I let the different tenor of the discussion prevent me from using this analysis with The Boys directly. CRT was still a motivation for my questioning, but at the time I did not see the need to use it to challenge these teachers. Instead, what became forefront was a discussion of possibility. We talked about what teachers who desire to work against institutional racism can do to enact such a practice. In these conversations what became very pedagogical to me was that educators (teachers and those in academia both) could use language that is very hopeful. In this respect, this dialogue was very performative in the sense that a performance perspective of critical ethnography illuminates "what could be" and not just "what is" (Madison, 2005, p. 5).

Using more language that reflected a critical (versus liberal) understanding of racial disparity, Elijah and John were much more vocal in the discussions than the third teacher, David, who often did not speak much until the other two had left the table to get something to eat or drink. While they both spoke with language that was filled with hope and possibility, David was open about his struggles in working with poorer African American students and his comments represented language that is more typical of what I have heard from white pre-service teachers and other white in-service teachers, language that may still promote racial equity but that also adheres to liberal interpretations of that racism. Interestingly enough, David was the only one of the three who intended to continue teaching. At the time, neither John and Elijah thought they would be teaching the following year (though John did end up continuing to teach). They saw much more possibility in their social justice work outside of the teaching profession. So, David's language often had the effect of bringing the conversation back to the seemingly more mundane aspects of classroom dynamics and the certainly more problematic aspects of race and teaching.

> David: Kids, it just doesn't seem like they care. I think it's whether black, white, it doesn't matter. I mean when kids just act like they don't care, it's a negative for me.

Despite such comments, this set of interviews was the most performative in the sense that Elijah and John, who were much more vocal, presented possibilities of how teachers with social justice motivations could talk and act. They were performing their social justice selves, the aspects of their identities that were concerned with anti-racist thought and practice. Both Elijah and John were very astute about how racism is perpetuated in society generally and in school more specifically. Furthermore, both of them tried to enact antiracist practice in their classes. To a large extent, this had the effect of them seeing themselves as outsiders to a certain degree. Interestingly, this outsider status was something they also saw in their childhoods as well. They narrated stories about how they came to think the way they do. Throughout the conversations, I had a hard time more critically analyzing these teachers' views, but when challenges did arise, they were often sparked by comments David made. In this way, he proved to be a functional and even necessary counterweight to the hope and possibility that Elijah and John exuded.

RACIAL CONSCIOUSNESS: EMOTION AND THE POSSIBILITY OF ANTIRACIST EDUCATION

As I mentioned above, the conversations started in a different place from the other interviews in the study. Early on, however, I did ask the boys about colorblindness and what they thought of the concept.

> John: It just makes me wonder what angle that term's being used. Like (a) people aren't really colorblind. They are definitely affected by people's color, whether it's conscious or unconscious. And (b) I guess the flip side to that is would be that people tend to treat certain races as invisible. They are blind to people of a different color and don't really perceive their entire humanity.
>
> Ben: It sounds like it's not a practice or ideology that either of you believe in.
>
> John: Not a bit.
>
> Elijah: Because it's not a reality. … Here at Central High School, really anywhere, it's something that… race is so evident and in your face that at times the person sees somebody as their race. So there really is no way to subscribe to colorblindness.

These comments exemplify the importance John and Elijah put on seeing and acknowledging racial difference. They were also able to articulate both how racism exists in a structural, institutional manner and how liberal ideology supports these structures. Subsequently they were aware of how white teachers like themselves were complicit in those structures.

> John: I think there's a lot of teachers at our school that definitely try to be aware of race and take a very vehement stance to be proponents of that race and…those are people who tend not to blinded by culture, but really conscious and forcing themselves to address it, and then there's also people who are completely blinded by it, and I definitely think that there's racism. You know, racism is present. It's prevalent. It's not free from the doors of Central High School. Institutionally speaking, I think just the way that we structure our teaching that there is complete lack of equity, and I think it is racist in its nature for us to not equalize our resources. You know, our greatest resource as public schools is our teachers, in theory. Teachers are our greatest resources, and it we truly believed in equity, then our greatest teachers, our most experienced teachers, would be teaching students of all races, and it wouldn't just be the teachers that have been there the longest, are supposedly the best teachers, teaching just AP classes. That's kind of my biggest beef with just equity and latent institutional racism, at least at Central High.

John, before even reading or discussing CRT with me, was able to articulate complicity using the connection between structural racism and property. He understood that access to valuable resources, such as good teachers, was affected by race.

Elijah and John's racial consciousness—the fact that race was on their minds a lot already—moved us much more quickly into their views on colorblindness and the existence of institutional racism in school and teacher practice to what they personally do to combat the those practices. For both Elijah and John, this consisted of thinking and talking about teaching in humanistic, emotional terms. Their primary motivations in teaching went beyond academic learning and certainly beyond any sense of doing well on tests or academic objectives

> John: Being able to, in art, experience the other point of view…being able to see a different side of humanity and to understand their tragedy and their pain and their suffering and their oppressive history without having to go through it, to be able to vicariously through the role of a character—perhaps within art and theater—feel it. We have to feel what it is to be someone else. We can't just learn about it and regurgitate the data about what is and what has been through the curriculum but to feel it.
>
> Elijah: It has to be emotional.
>
> John: It's only human empathy and emotion that will really empower people to want to change things.

According to Giroux (1997), as liberal discourse does not position societal institutions such as schools as cultural in any political way, liberal ideology promotes equality through an adherence to the structures of society as they exist currently. Success and equality in education will come through following the structures (i.e., the processes and modes of categorization) that exist in schools. For Elijah and John, these structures did not address a fundamental aspect of what education should be. For them, a prime part of education was for emotional, not academic, development. In addition, they connected the achievement of racial equity with this emotional development. Thus, the modes for success and equity that they employed resisted liberal interpretations of racial change (or any kind of equity) as occurring through current teaching and curricular practices that focused on academic senses of intelligence and were rather linked to the development of their students' ability to tap into their feeling, affective selves. Elijah articulated this through talk of connecting to people emotionally, about changing people's hearts.

> Elijah: Who wants to suffer? Nobody. And who wants to change the way they are through suffering, through feeling pain? No one physically. But if we can do that in the four walls of the classroom... how do you make a kid feel somehow less painful while—for the sake of I'm not going to harm you or hurt you—and in order to actually see what's going on here you need to feel pain. You need to feel it, but it's all cerebral. This kind of idea of moving head or moving heart John and I talked about. But how do you move heart? You can't do it with just words. You can have the best speeches but if it's not well spoken, with passion, then it's mute. So, the role of the teacher is to try to find a way to be emotional… how can you bring emotion into the class or how can you get these experiences. You can change hearts. If you get to someone's heart in one day, you get them forever.

Later when I discuss how these teachers identified themselves as antiracist educators, I will show where Elijah's desire to "move heart" came from and on what this means to him. For now, I think it is important to note that Elijah and John were the teachers in this study who used language that most closely adhered to my preconceived notions of what critical antiracist practice consisted of. By that I mean that they held a critical understanding of how racism is institutionalized and talked about how they tried to oppose that in their practice. The other teachers in the study certainly gave me insight into what it could look like and may have been as effective in teaching their students of color, but Elijah and John articulated versions of antiracist education that was most overtly critical of liberal interpretations of the institutional racism and of the institution itself. The interviews with them brought out a detailed wording of their philosophies of education, which included a critically antiracist mission.

For John, art and to a certain extent nature were key concepts and practices that helped him articulate his mode of resisting traditional interpretation of education. To repeat and extend the quote that opened this chapter:

> John: I think art is also one of those tools that is incredibly educational to see the better side and experience true creativity and expression of humanity. I think there's just something magical that lives in the ability to open your spirit up to art, poetry—you know and see with poetic eyes. When you see with poetic eyes you look at the beauty and the hope and the potential of humanity and not just the history and way it is and how it's securing your privileged state. Just two weeks ago I was at Washington, DC with students and one of the students just made an incredible poetic observation to me that just rocked my world. We were at the steps of the Lincoln Memorial and he said, "Wow, how ironic!" and you looked up and there were six black men sweeping the ice off the steps of the Lincoln Memorial. It just made you really look at like how really freed were black people from slavery, has it really just transformed into classism? …I think you have to be willing to look at the nature of reality from something other than a legislative standpoint, you know from its more…the undercurrents of poetically what is really going on in the world, and communicating with people outside of the realm of just regular legislative, practical language.

John believed that using art and performance with his students enabled them to see the world both critically and with a sense of social justice. At several times in the interviews, he commented on how art helped him move conversations from "practical" language to what he termed here as "seeing with poetic eyes." Though he did not use the term liberalism, I interpret the kind of language John hopes to use with and instill in his students to be one that breaks free of liberal interpretations of the way the world needs to be. He sees a real possibility of social change with such language.

> John: …kids who go through it, kids who are a part of our shows,[1] the kids who work with outward bound, the different programs that I work with where they're engaging with people of a different race and they're engaging in very societally aware issues within the context of that program… they've shown that they learn that it's something that should be brought to the forefront of their consciousness. There's not a whole lot of people who engage in something that's very moving and empathetic in its nature and just totally ignore it. I've seen it work incredibly successfully in my arts and theater and in the outward bound crews that I've worked with and kids that I take on hiking trips. And nature is another one of those arenas that I think is incredibly effective for just being a space for people to learn what the… I think nature is the art of place in a sense. It is a blank canvas. Everything's working harmoniously together, in perfect rhythmic circles, and there's no real laws of inferiority and superiority. It's all kind of working together, and I think that just creates a space that's a very unique, pure space for conversations about the absurdity of hierarchies that take place.

Nature was very much a liminal space in John's eyes. Like art, it could be used to get students to be aware of something important beyond the day-to-day structures (like the hierarchies he mentions above) that play on their lives. I failed to ask him what happens to students when they leave such spaces and return to the less artistic spaces of their everyday lives and failed to ask about how art and nature could be used more to promote antiracism in the current structures of schools. I do not want to downplay the hope and possibility that Elijah and John see through such views of education, but I do think it is important to put that hope in context.

Sometimes, the teachers themselves added this context in the interviews. Despite all the hope Elijah and John saw with students and getting them to see, these teachers were somewhat more pessimistic about how this change in vision could work with teachers. Though they admitted to working with some teachers who were highly racially conscious, they also acknowledged that some teachers are not. Furthermore, they pointed out that various structures of the institution of education made it hard for teachers to adhere to antiracist educational practices.

> Elijah: The problem with No Child Left Behind, and that's the problem that with teachers, we view our success in changing achievement through scores, and that's just [indicates a lot of frustration]... that might happen eventually, but if you judge your success on that, it's very frustrating... and you can be blinded by what's actually more important...you're not going to judge success for 10 or 15 or 20 years about how they have been affected, in effect about how they handle themselves with their families, their companies, their job. And so whereas I hope that I am changing people to think about society, think about class, think about themselves, and their role in their world, if you don't see changes in the numbers that the school gives you credit for at the end of every year, you could have the most rock solid lesson plan about helping out this kid right here, and you may not do well on the tests, and nothing's changed in that respect, but he goes home happy that day, the next day he might come in a little early with a smile on his face... so it's difficult to judge success.
>
> John: And that's administratively one of the main things that's fucked up is that...we're teaching in this construct where that's the primary focus and it almost reinforces to the *teachers* that it's not important to desire to bring about some ethical, emotional growth within students.

For John, the prevalent ideology that drives schools did not support teaching for ethical, emotional growth. Teachers who wanted to promote such growth are in a difficult situation because this humanistic approach resists the sanctioned and assessed purposed of education in public schools. Elijah pointed out that standards-based and standardized testing movements like No Child Left Behind only made such a humanistic approach harder to implement. Schools do not give credit for how much a teacher can get a student to smile, for example. His comment about helping out "this kid right here" indicated that his motivation also does not adhere to a narrow and solely academic conceptualization of success but rather on some sense of social consciousness. Both Elijah and John talked about the frustration they felt because of how the structures of school hindered such a consciousness as the major motivation in education.

In addition, both John and especially Elijah (the teacher who was most quickly leaving the teaching profession) talked about the personal challenges they faced as teachers with more explicit approaches to equitable pedagogy. Both had heard people talk about them as "anti-white."

> John: You know, [a student] was just telling me the other day—his girlfriend is white, he's black—and he was saying, "Lara, why don't you go watch the game in John's room?" And she said, "John doesn't like white people." And that to me was just totally my anti-creed.

Elijah also had examples of comments that labeled him as anti-white, and these were said to him directly.

> Elijah: "If you're going to promote this [i.e., non-white] race, aren't you doing at the expense of other people [i.e., whites] as well?" "Shouldn't you take just as much passion and pride in the contributions and successes of every person, including white people?" "Are you racist against white people?"
>
> Ben: You've heard that?
>
> Elijah: Yeah.

One the bases for this type of reaction is that many whites see society and schools as absent of color, and Elijah and John recognized the existence of this view. These whites did not see the norms of school as white, so when Elijah and John focus on color, these whites (both teachers and students) assumed that Elijah and John are "anti-white." These two teachers acknowledged that they go out of their way for students of color and taught curricula that highlight non-white histories and perspectives, and they recognized that this invoked the perception that they are against whites.

> John: And kids have a hard time... like a lot of kids maybe perceive my approach as like an affirmative action curriculum. Because black people have been so disenfranchised throughout history, I find it almost necessary to compensate for that. Not to undermine and minimize the effect that I want to have on white kids, but I want to put my net effort into trying to lift up kids who have been disadvantaged. And subsequently I think a lot of white kids have perceived that I don't like white people.

Elijah made comments that indicated that he had received similar reactions from both students and teachers for focusing on the "disadvantaged." When I asked them where such attitudes come from, they both had a response.

> Elijah: Many forces. [We both laugh.] I think one could be white guilt. Another could be there's a just an effort to try to correct past wrongs through a kind of affirmative action or affirmative teaching, actions towards trying to include, and they [whites] see it as, "Why aren't you coming to meet me?" where the "me" is an individual. And of course history... because everyone's

> selfish, you have to talk about me. If you're going to talk about somebody else, then why don't you talk about me, too?
>
> John: And it's largely new. You think about how long it's been since civil rights. Taking a stand for African Americans as white people, granted it might be a couple of generations old, but as far as progressive teaching methods have been implemented, it's still a very new era.

The teachers and students they were referring to clung to an interpretation of the school as an institution that was colorless. Such a view adheres to liberal ideology that claims whites and non-whites have the same chances in institutions such as schools. So, when these teachers acted in ways that focus on race, it was seen as unfair because it was going against the colorblind structure of schooling. However, both Elijah and John, as I pointed out before, saw the dominant structures of schooling as linked to whiteness. Thus, they knew that whites had an advantage that had to be overcome, and they each tried to overcome this in their pedagogy and curricula, what Elijah termed "affirmative action or affirmative teaching." Elijah and John's direction of effectivity was thus anti-liberal and their modes of effectivity came out in their teaching and choices of curricula.

Engaging in such resistant modes of effectivity had an effect on these two teachers. They each discussed the challenge to doing this kind of work, and I asked them about the success of their work. Elijah replied once, "It makes me want to quit." John was more hopeful in his response. He had been at this school for several years and saw that currently there were more teachers who he could work with, more who "share a lot of the same values" with him as compared to when he started at Central High School. Yet even with his optimism, he believed there was something fundamentally wrong with how school was structured.

> John: It's hard to sustain the importance of something that is positive and progressive when they're not getting it anywhere else, which is why it's important, speaking here, to bring allies of teachers who are trying to fight for a lot of these same things together. I think we need, in order to really impress some of these differences, a completely… not just hoping there are a bunch of teachers who are all trying to reach kids in this way, but some more structure to humanistic approach to education, more multiculturalism through collaborative teaching in education, like having a student going through interactive exercises in history, English, and humanities, into science, into math, and having both the content and the process all being centrally grounded in the same humanistic approach, to where it's sustained throughout their day, so that maybe in hopes even if they are in a racist, classist, sexist context at home that that sustaining voice from school will be the grounding voice in their life.

On the one hand, John believed he had allies to work with and was hopeful about bringing more along to make his approach to education more successful. On the other hand, a widespread approach to humanistic and collaborative multicultural education was still something that did not exist in the school. In other parts of the conversation, he made similar remarks on how insufficient he thought the school's approach to equity was. Combined with the discussion about the personal comments they have both received, they both portrayed a strong sense of frustration.

The two teachers continued to follow their own approaches, at least to some extent, despite the challenges they faced. They would maybe leave the profession, but they would not change the way they taught or thought.

> Elijah: You just kind of move into your conscious and you just kind of move forward with one more thought, and you just strive to do what you're doing. You try not to offend anybody really. That's what you're trying to do.

> John: I don't really care. You know it's like, if you're going to take a stand for people who haven't had an enormous stand taken for them, people are going to see it, they're going to absorb it, they're going to be responsive to it, you know. But I'm not going to let my action be controlled by other people's emotions that can't really see the entire big picture. And if anything that tells me, it reinforces to me that, "Oh shit, people see what I'm trying to fight for." Even if they're seeing it like I'm the wrong side and I don't like white people, at least they're seeing that here's a white person who is trying to fight for equal education for blacks.

There was a sense of isolation that I got from these comments. John at least used the resistance he experienced to make allies and to fight this isolation. Elijah, on the other hand, was more affected by the isolation in the sense that he was not able to stick with teaching as long. For both of these teachers, and even for David to some extent, positioning themselves as against the mainstream was where they saw themselves as social justice educators and this outsider status was a large part of their identities.

OUTSIDER IDENTITY

The sense of being outsiders, or different from most of the people they taught with, extended beyond the school. In talking about how these teachers came to their perspectives on race and equity, we discussed their personal histories. For John, his outsider status was strongly linked to his desire to teach differently, to follow a humanistic approach to education.

> John: And I think one of the difficult things for me as a teacher…this is a criticism that I used to house much more of the beginning of my teaching at Central High that I don't now, and part of me wonders if that's because working with more people like you [referring to Elijah] who share a lot of the same values, but I used to become really frustrated on just sustaining the idea of some of the things that I was trying to impress with my kids. Like, all of the things that we talked about. Like having a more humanistic approach to education… So it used to really frustrate me, but not to toot my horn, but to be like one of the only teachers I would see on a regular basis who was trying to impress this shit into kids, and then you've got kids for 55 minutes a day

> and you're trying to affect their hearts and minds and enough to the point where they're going to see some of the value in it, but then they go out and then they get 5 other teachers who are just shoving data down their throats, you know. It's hard to sustain the importance of something that is positive and progressive when they're not getting it anywhere else, which is why it's important, speaking here, to bring allies of teachers who are trying to fight for a lot of these same things together.

Life was better at Central High because there were more teachers who he saw as allies, but there was still some sense of isolation in John's words. Even with his allies, he was on the outside of a system of education that did not support his humanistic approach. At the same time, he was able to talk about the difficulty in a very positive way. He saw the possibility of bringing more allies on board to his approach.

John was very similarly positive in talking about how he was positioned as an outsider in his childhood.

> John: I personally grew up all up and down the east coast. I never went to one school for more than a year until I got to high school. I lived in a lot of black areas. I spent a lot of time in Detroit. And I never really knew anybody. And not really knowing anybody I grew up as a child observing human behavior a lot, and I really love my parents for that. You know the fact that I was forced to be put into educational systems where I had to just—constantly every year growing up—watch everybody and just see like who I would really be connected and attached with, and I think I afforded myself an opportunity to see and perceive better, more angelic forms of human nature, and the more shallow forms of human nature, in people as a child through that experience. And… I didn't really prosper because of class. I didn't really prosper a whole lot because of grades. And I also just love the underdog as you said. Why are we here if we're not here to help people who need it?

John articulated his isolation (i.e., his "not knowing anybody") as a source of learning. He learned how to observe not just human behavior but "angelic" forms of human behavior and, and he was able to learn how to connect himself to such behavior. He also attributed his love of the underdog to his outsider, observer status. Instead of being resentful for such a position, he thanked his parents for it.

He gave the same positive sense of being able to connect to people currently in his personal life. At this time, however, instead of being forced into an outsider position as he was as a child, he chose it by seeking out practices that open him up to new experiences and people. John included art, performance, and nature—which I already discussed to certain extent—in his approach to teaching as ways to connect to his students and to a social justice agenda. They were similarly a part of his personal life. He even mentioned the occasional use of certain drugs to connect him to that sense of openness to people and experiences.

> John: I mean, it's kind of a funny side note you know that psychedelic drugs—LSD, mushrooms, marijuana, whatever have you—historically

> speaking you find hippy movements centered around social justice. That definitely isn't the main source of where it comes from but it's kind of one of those tools that people use that...expands the mind. It's an open form of being. It's a collective kind of being under those influences. They may teach people through experiences that it's fun to be open, peace-loving, warm, loving everybody, and then you expand those experiences to the everyday practices of your life.

For John, being open and self-reflexive helped also to lead him to being critical in the sense that he wanted to critique and work against what he called the "shallow forms of human nature."

Elijah also discussed an openness to people different from himself as being rooted in his upbringing. Like with John, experiences and privileges that gave him contact with people culturally different from himself taught him to see himself as different from other whites.

> Elijah: ...my experience in New York City, when I was in a school that was probably 90% minorities—Asian, urban Latino, African American—and that became the norm for me. I think that and in college as well and in my reading, I've been more attracted to the plight of people, and so here that culminates in rooting for Latinos and African Americans, those who are underachieving and the achievement gap.

Feagin and O'Brien (2003) talk about how whites have been affected because of having had significant relationships with people of color. For Elijah, he saw those relationships from his childhood as affecting who he is today. He connected these experiences to his sense of racial equity now.

What was somewhat different from John's experience was that Elijah also had a sense of class privilege that John did not. For one, he had intellectual, academic, progressive parents that taught him more directly about social justice.

> Elijah: They were from a very conservative, white, Christian town in Iowa. And so immediately they were kind of "root for the underdog"—they were Jesse Jackson supporters when he came to town—very intellectual. And I think they also took interest in it. And they were just more "shoot for the underdog." I think that's where the passion starts. And that just happened to be black Americans.

According to Elijah, his parents always fought for the equity of African Americans, so he learned to do the same. In addition, he had wealthy grandparents that influenced him in a somewhat different way.

> Elijah: Along that same question, I also had grandparents who were fairly affluent in southern sections of Chicago. So, I'd go to a country club, and see people of color serving me, and the norm was they had to kiss my ass even at 12 years old or my grandfather wouldn't tip them. And I asked why is it this way? And some people just turn a blind eye. I can see where it is very easy to grow up always to see people of color serving you. It is very difficult to

> reverse those who are in positions…and I see this with my girlfriend and coming to her house. She's an au pair and so…I can at least not be blinded by whiteness.

Instead of turning a blind eye, his influence from his parents and his significant relationships with people of color (including his current girlfriend, who is Brazilian) have helped him not be blinded by his own privilege and whiteness. Elijah positioned himself as different from most whites, who were not able to "not be blinded."

Elijah also saw himself as an outsider in the sense of not being from the south. Neither John nor David actually grew up in the south, but they had been in North Carolina much longer. For Elijah, it was only his second year, and he spoke about southerners with some disdain.

> Elijah: I think when you talk about racism in the past, oppression in the past, some students see that as you are speaking harshly of them as people. You're saying, "You, white man, you did the wrong." And, especially kids who grew from the south so to speak, and I say this as an outsider, I don't use the word "we," I use the word "white southerners" or "white slave owners" and they know their history and they might literally be in touch with their past, too, and sometimes it comes down on them. So, it can be offensive in the way you say it.

Elijah understood that his remarks about southerners offended his white southern students, and this was one of the instances of when he did not include himself in the "we" that was complicit in the institutional racism he sees. At other times he did put himself in the category with most whites—such as when he claimed that more African American teachers were needed because there were certain experiences that whites could never understand. However, since this was an instance when Elijah seemed to divert his own responsibility for the re-inscription of discrimination, it was one of the few times in these interviews that I actually tried to challenge one of The Boys. Even with my challenge, Elijah positions himself as different from most white teachers and talks about the "southern pride" he senses from other teachers at his school.

Despite his remarks about southerners, Elijah for the most part did recognize his own racial and class privilege. It enabled him to understand why whites want to maintain their privilege, even if he personally did not want to use it in the same way.

> Elijah: It's interesting people with privilege. If I was rich, and I can see where a parent would say, "Just keep my kid safe. It's better this way. You're not going to really change the world, but at least you can be safe, you can be happy, you can be well." I just can't blame a parent for that in some ways. But I guess I just don't see the world in that way.

Elijah was able to distance himself the way he believed most whites maintained their privilege. By positioning himself outside of that group of whites, Elijah narrated himself as a socially just, antiracist white teacher. In fact, it is itself a privilege whites have to be able to distance ourselves from our racial categorizations. Similarly, even though John was more positive about finding allies, he—like Elijah—also positioned himself on the outside of a mainstream white identity.

What was educative for me from talking to Elijah and John—as a white educator who also has the privilege of positioning himself outside the mainstream of his own racial categorization, in itself a privilege of whiteness—was how whites could position ourselves as outside the mainstream in order to enact antiracist agendas. At least Elijah and John used their outsider status to create teaching practices that could work against the institutional racism they saw. Talking with Elijah and John gave me hope for how whites teachers could, rather than deny their racial privilege, instead use an understanding of that privilege to construct potentially antiracist practices. I do not want to overstate how much Elijah and John were able to do or how much I have been able to learn, but talking with them about their outsider identities has helped me think more about how to approach teachers about challenging racism in their practice.

OUTLIER AND COUNTERWEIGHT

I have so far not said much about David, and that is in part due to that I was unsure of how to include him in this chapter. He was quiet most of the time that Elijah and John spoke in the interviews. He seemed to listen and take the discussion in. In addition, he was in many senses sort of an outlier with the group. He was a little older than the other two teachers (in his early forties), he was teaching longer (just over 15 years) and except for when talking about testing he did not position himself as an outsider to mainstream education in the same way. Rather, most of his comments, which came after Elijah and John had left or were at least away from the table, focused on the daily aspects of teaching and in particular his interactions with his students of color. He was the only one of the three who talked extensively about frustrations with his students.

> David: The whole part about being engaged. I want them to be engaged in part of the conversation. It's important to me. Kids, it just doesn't seem like they care. I think it's whether black, white, it doesn't matter. I mean when kids just act like they don't care, it's a negative for me.

In addition, where Elijah and John almost never spoke negatively of their students of color—their frustrations came from other teachers or the white students that they saw as more privileged—David did talk about the difficulty he had in working with some of his African American students.

As I indicated earlier in this chapter, David certainly had a good heart, and he often positioned himself as similar to Elijah and John in his motivation for teaching.

> David: You know when I…I've made it very clear to them that I hate standardized tests, but I don't have a standardized test [his subject area does not require one]. I'm in a very lucky position. I'm teaching them about the earth. I'm teaching topics that will be valuable to them when they grow up

> and have to make decisions. You know some of them [the students] might be in a position to make major decisions. They happen to have the background. So, I'm motivated by my desire to teach about the earth.

Here, David, an earth science teacher, articulated a similar humanistic agenda for his teaching: e.g., "I'm teaching them about the earth." He was not concerned with tests (and admitted he was lucky that he did not have to be in his course as there was no end-of-course test) and wanted the students to learn something from his course that might contribute to the social good. He shared the same frustration as Elijah and John about the traditional and sanctioned approaches to education. While he was perhaps less articulate about a social justice agenda in his teaching, he still taught from a motivation that goes beyond academic performance. At the same time, along with his commitment to teach about the environment and all of the admiration he had for Elijah and John's approach to education, David articulated his views on racial disparity most closely to the thinking of liberal ideology. Most of these views came out when he discussed his African American students. I got the sense that he wanted to do well for his African American students—several times he told me that he had a good rapport with "the black kids"—and that he wanted to resist singling that group out, but he did discuss these students in a way that signaled their actions as contrary to the appropriate norms of the school.

For example, there were a few times in our conversation where David singled out his African American students' behavior. Perhaps the prime example came when he discussed teaching in an after-school program designed to helped students who had failed the state mandated end of course tests.

> David: I had a huge struggle with that [program]. About two thirds of the class was African American girls, 9th grade. And I don't teach 9th grade or even 10th graders. It's usually juniors and seniors, and these girls were loud, very loud, and even if you separated them, they always found each other… This is [their] second chance to get [their] grade raised from an F to a D or whatever, and you know if people are even a minute late, you're out. There were these rules and you have to have perfect attendance. And I found that I wasn't really supported in trying to enforce those rules.

David talked about his attempt to strictly follow the rules of attendance and lateness and his frustration with how difficult it was for him to do that. In the conversation he commented on the African American girls that he had in class, that they were the ones who did not follow the rules. He talked about how he understood that these girls might have had a different learning style, but he also talked about how he thought they had to at least sometimes adapt their style for the benefit of his other students. Interestingly, when I asked him how many students he was specifically referring to, he indicated that these girls made up half the class (as opposed to the two-thirds claim he made earlier). So, he wanted these 10 African American girls to adapt to what he perceived the learning style of the remaining 10 students, a combination of African American male and white male and female students.

From a critical race standpoint, David did not acknowledge, and I did not question him on, the whiteness involved in either the rules he wanted to enforce or what he considered to be the appropriate learning style for a high school classroom. I do not want to deny that these girls may have presented certain challenges, especially since I did not observe the class. Rather, I want to point out that the only he time talked about specific students in racial terms was to point out when they did not adhere to a certain notion of appropriate behavior and that in these cases he used in negative terms to describe them. In contrast, when he talked about his good rapport with black students, he never provided specific examples. I am reminded of Guinier and Torres' (2002) discussion of racial synecdoche. David's commentary about these girls is an example of how many whites often depict specific blacks as representative of the entire black race, especially when that depiction is negative. David did not narrate his "well-behaved" black students as representative of all blacks (rather, they were the exception), nor did he depict "poorly-behaved" whites as representative of all whites. Again, I do not want to position David as intentionally promoting racial disparity. The fact that David chose to teach in the after school program is some evidence that he wanted to work towards racial equity in some way. I do believe, however, that his adherence to liberal notion of the school practices as culturally neutral (along with my failure to work with him to name the whiteness of those practices) prevented him from possibly realizing some of the equity he wanted to achieve.

David's comments about these girls and other minority students also influenced Elijah to talk about race in a more problematic way. For example, David's remarks on students who acted like they did not care sparked a conversation on motivation. At one point, Elijah showed some resistance to how much teachers should be responsible for motivating students.

> Elijah: How do you motivate? How long do you motivate until the point where the kid gets it? How many talks do you have with a kid before you inspire him or her and you get back in the classroom and you see no results?

So, while Elijah earlier discussed how school structures get in the way of what is important in education, here he placed the blame on students for not being motivated within such a structure. This somewhat contradicts his desire to "move heart" and adhered more to a liberal interpretation of change and success—i.e., that students have a structure that they can and should utilize in order to succeed. In addition, this conversation only came out when talking about what teachers can do to work more effectively with minority students.

John was the only teacher of the three to resist blaming minority students for the racial disparity they experience throughout the conversations. Rather than placing the blame on a lack of motivation on the students, he stuck with looking at how teachers and the current structure of schooling prevent teachers like himself from motivating students. Even though John resisted placing blame on minority students and looked for structural reasons that may instigate such feelings, David's discussion of kids not caring caused even John to highlight the difficulty in implementing a humanistic, anti-racist approach to education. So, in those few times David did speak when all three of the teachers were present, he often had the effect of being a counterweight for the hope Elijah and John presented and prompted them to focus on how the realities of the context in which they teach affect their humanistic, anti-racist goals.

An interesting observation I had in transcribing these interviews was how rarely I took up David's grounding of the conversation to examine more critically the hope and possibility that Elijah and John presented. I think a large part of why I found it difficult to challenge Elijah and John was because their articulations of racial consciousness matched mine. My motivation in the study was so much focused on getting white teachers to name the whiteness of their thoughts and practices that when I was presented with two teachers who already attempted to do that, I failed to examine how their whiteness and privilege still influenced how they thought and taught. I also realize, however, that other factors may have affected my ability to challenge as well; specifically, gender greatly influenced the tenor of our dialogue.

GENDER

I do remember at times in these interviews with The Boys thinking that I should be challenging some of their comments a bit more. After all, my position is that whites carry a racial privilege with us that comes out in ways that we do often see. In addition, my dialogic approach is to involve in a give and take so as we both may learn. Yet, I did not involve myself extensively in that give and take with The Boys and did not delve into the white privilege embedded in their comments, thoughts, and practices. As I mentioned above, part of my lack of examination stemmed from the fact that Elijah and John articulated racially consciousness in way similar to myself. That is not to say that their whiteness did not hinder their approaches to racial equity in any way, but as compared to the other teachers in this study they discussed race and white privilege that fit well with the language I use to talk about critically antiracist practice. I realize now that a large part of that convergence in our articulations was due to the ways we performed our antiracism is a particularly male style. The Boys' comments were often different from the women's in the study, and I heard their comments from a male gendered perspective. I allowed this to affect how I interviewed them.

Our male ways of performing our antiracist identities may have been be connected to our particularly male form of morality. Some research suggests that men and women work from different senses of morality—that women work from an ethic that centers care and men one that centers justice (Gilligan, 1982; Lyons, 1988). While this work has been heavily critiqued, I will use the construct—along with Connel's (1987) critique of it—to investigate the difference in The Boys' articulation of social justice and racial equity. Gilligan (1982) posited that morality for women stemmed from their connections to people. Women adapt concepts (including articulations of right and wrong) to work in the context of the people they know and care about. That does not mean that women have no belief in these concepts but rather that those beliefs and their articulations are highly interrelated to the relationships they have with specific people. Men, on the other hand, even when they talk about their attachments to people, base their senses of morality more directly on the concepts regardless of the how those concepts relate to the specific people in their lives.

Drawing from Gilligan's work, Lyons (1988) stated that "a morality of care appears to be a systematic, life-long concern of individuals" (p. 42). According to Lyons' research, women work more commonly from this care perspective. I tried to examine this difference between men and women in looking at the way in which the boys talked about social justice in relation to the women in the study. Sarah and Elizabeth certainly did mention specific students much more often than any of The Boys did. Sarah and Elizabeth readily came up with examples involving specific students that supported or challenged statements about race that I would make. The women in this study—especially Melissa and Sarah but even Elizabeth—presented their social justice educator selves just as much as The Boys did but did so in different ways. The women much more often told stories of specific students when I asked them how they either promote or fail to promote racial equity in the classroom. Thus, it was somewhat easier for me to analyze those examples. The Boys, on the other hand, used a much different language. At least to a certain extent, they spoke more about ideas, such as a humanistic approach to education or "moving heart," without often referencing specific students they know. Even when Elijah talks about "this kid right here" in an earlier quote, he is talking about a hypothetical rather than actual student. Since they rarely used specific examples from their classrooms (and I failed to elicit those examples from them) it was harder for me to delve into analyses of whether or not their practices promoted racial equity in a critical way or not. When I did ask questions it was more for them to clarify themselves or to ask about their motivations in developing their stances on race and antiracism.

At the same time, Gilligan's (1982) hypothesis does not hold up completely with either the men or the women in the study. Connell (1987) sees such paradigms as over-deterministic and proposes that several forms of sexual character emerge in the same society at the same time and that "multiple femininities and masculinities are…a central fact about gender and the way its structures are lived" (pp. 63–64). Thus, it is a bit too simple to say that Sarah and Elizabeth's visions of social justice stemmed solely from their relationships with their specific students and that The Boys' versions ignored theirs. For example, Elizabeth was very able at speaking about complicity on a conceptual level. Likewise, John did talk about a few of his students specifically and did so with care. What I find useful about Gilligan's thesis is that it provides me an entry point into examining the difference between these women's and men's formulations of their social justice work and helps shed some light on why I failed to challenge the men as much as I did the women generally speaking.

This is not all to say that I could not have questioned The Boys more. Certainly their comments could be interpreted more critically. As their language was so conceptual at times, I could have tried to ground it in more specific examples from their daily classroom practice and juxtapose their claims of critically antiracist practice with counterexamples from that practice. I did not do that, however, and in that way I performed my male gender as well. I let myself stay on the conceptual level and only talked about specific circumstances and students when they were brought up. Even when David's comments did move the conversation into the more concrete world of daily practice, I followed the tone set by Elijah and John.

This may have been in part because of my jealousy of the ways in which Elijah and John were able to pay attention to race in their teaching. Perhaps I wished that I had been able to focus on race in my teaching as explicitly as they did, or at least as they did in their articulations of their practice. So, I was somewhat preoccupied with also presenting my own identity as an antiracist white male to The Boys. I did not feel the need to narrate my antiracist identity in the same way with either Melissa, Sarah or Elizabeth, who were all as outspoken as Elijah and John and who all consciously worked towards racial equity. With these women, the presentation of myself as a social justice, anti-racist educator came when I probed into their thinking. With Elijah and John, on the other hand, I showed that aspect of my identity to position myself as an equal, as someone who could hang with people who I thought were doing good work, who could be me to a certain extent, and who were doing more than me to some extent. I was performing a form of male solidarity, a white male solidarity. I positioned the group—and myself as part of that group—as "outsider whites" who "get it." In other words, I positioned us as an exceptional group of white males who, unlike most whites, understood racism and were able to combat it. While we may have been closer to pursuing an antiracist agenda than many other whites, we certainly engaged in that agenda as males. Furthermore, the women in this study, and Melissa and Sarah in particular, adhered to antiracism much more than most teachers I have worked with.

To better show respect the commitment to discuss race that the women in this study have shown, I need to acknowledge how my gendered way of conducting research has positioned them. However, acknowledgement is just a start. The next steps for me are to interrogate my own male privilege and to include gender analysis in my future work. After all, a main characteristic of CRT is intersectionality (Guinier & Torres, 2002; Delgado & Stefancic, 2001; Matsuda et al, 1993). CRT focuses on race analysis not only to uncover racism but also all forms of marginalization, including those stemming from male privilege.

CONCLUSION

In spite of, or perhaps because of, the gendered nature of our performance, the conversation with The Boys was filled with a hope not present in the other interviews. That is not to say that racial equity was not seen as an incredibly difficult goal to achieve but rather that two of these teachers did at least see ways to work towards that goal despite its difficulty. So, what was particularly educative for me about the hope they expressed was that it was evidence that some white teachers do acknowledge the structural forms of racism that exist in schools and do engage in practice that counters liberal interpretations of and solutions to racial disparity. In fact, looking back at my conversations with the women, and especially Melissa and Sarah, I wonder if I could not have also had similar conversations with them. Each of those women also had critical understandings of racial disparity and worked at antiracism in critical ways. At the times of those conversations, due to our gendered ways of dialoguing, I was more focused on the liberal remnants of their comments and practices and on using CRT to examine those aspects.

I can only speculate how using CRT in a dialogic fashion would have affected our conversation. I would hope that it would add depth to the explication of racially conscious thought and practice that Elijah and John presented. I could imagine having talked with them about how their pedagogical and curricular decisions affect—both positively and negatively—their minority students' access to curriculum, resources, and an equal education. Such analysis would not have to deny the work that teachers such as John, Elijah, Melissa and Sarah do towards racial equity, nor would it necessarily eliminate the hope that they express. Instead, more critical analysis done with teachers who are striving to achieve antiracist goals might actually help them better realize those goals because it might better get them to connect the way they articulate their antiracist identities to the racial realities that exist in their schools and classrooms. Thus, such critical analysis could draw on their racial consciousness—and in fact deepen it—in order to affect their daily practice with students.

I would also hope that using CRT analysis would help influence David to draw on the similarities he does have with Elijah and John in order to confront some of the liberal aspects of his racial understanding and develop thinking and practice that counters racism in more critical ways. Perhaps if I had interviewed David individually in addition to with the other men, I would have been able to discuss his thinking with him more in the ways I did with Elizabeth or Stephanie. In fact, had I interviewed each of these men separately, I might have been able to problematize the "outsider white" identity I helped construct. I do believe there is value to examining how The Boys' sense of outsider status helps them envision and enact critically antiracist practice. However, I also think that status needs to be analyzed more deeply for its connection to privilege. The Boys and I have the racial *and* gender privilege to be outsiders to the cultural groups to which we belong. Even though Elijah and John got negative reactions from some of the whites they worked with, they also got to claim a certain amount of clout as whites who "get it," and I can make a similar claim. A more thorough analysis—e.g., using CRT to name the whiteness of and the actions that stem from our privileged claims—could have helped me analyze how our positionality makes us complicit in institutional racism in our own ways. In essence, I could have better uncovered the colorblindness that still existed in The Boys' and my thoughts and actions.

Furthermore, using similar discussions on antiracist and outsider identities and motivations with the female teachers in this study might have helped me enrich my analysis with them. First of all, it may have helped me better highlight additional facets of how these women were already resistant to liberal ideological interpretations of race and racism. By understanding more where they were coming from (i.e., how thy positioned themselves in relation to the dominant discourse of race and schooling), I might have been able to see the ways in which their thoughts and actions were already motivated by critical understandings of racial equity, or at least to better see how they had the potential to be. Secondly, I might have been able to then draw on their deeper antiracist motivations and their often acute racial understandings to better learn from the analysis I did do with them. After all, what

I was able to do with the women, I could not (or did not) with the men. Namely, I was able to analyze aspects of teacher thought and practice that supported institutional racism. We did this through naming the whiteness connected to those practices and discussing complicity. So, in many ways, the interviews with the women were more true to my own research agenda and were more educative with regards of how to talk with teachers about complicity. I will need to continue to investigate further why I was able to do this with the women and why I did not do it with the men, so in future work I can be attuned to both the problematic comments men make and the more positive and pedagogical ones from women. Perhaps by discussing the women's sense of identity with regard to racial awareness, I could have learned how they developed their antiracist motivations. An understanding of such motivations could potentially be helpful in working with teachers towards developing the analytical skills that are needed to understand and combat institutional racism.

Even though I did not conduct a deeper analysis of our particularly gendered whiteness with The Boys, I can at least focus on the fact that white teachers can have beliefs that counter dominant ideology and that they can also discuss how to resist that ideology in practice. The Boys' astute understanding of the structures that cause racial disparity and prevent teachers from performing their anti-racist selves was complimented by their ability to articulate, and even practice, critically antiracist ways of being. While I do not want to overstate the extent to which these teachers countered the effect of school racism, from a teacher educator perspective their stories do provide examples that I can share with future students as their stories can help me articulate potentially anti-racist practice.

NOTES

1 John and his students put together spoken-word and dramatic performances that draw on the *Theater of the Oppressed* (1979) work of Augusto Boal.

CHAPTER 6

MOVING HEART

The Pedagogical Potential of Critical Race Theory

To an extent, the narrative chapters and the series of interviews in this study build on each other. As one of the goals of performance ethnography is for the research to be pedagogical (Denzin, 2003), I organized the chapters to illustrate more or less linear progression of what I learned from the study. In Chapter 2, I learned the issues central to the study. Namely, colorblindness exists in complex and contradictory ways in teachers' thinking and practice. In addition, this colorblindness is linked to a liberal ideology that still exists in aspects of schooling. From Stephanie, I both learned to expound on these issues and to begin to understand how CRT can be used to fight the racist aspects of colorblindness and liberalism. With Melissa's help, I was able to being to see more clearly what a CRT analysis could look like with teachers. So from these two initial interviews, I learned about CRT and was able to find a language to put CRT in the context of teacher practice.

I deepened my understanding of this analysis in the interviews with Sarah in Chapter 3. Her motivation to learn enabled us to delve into specific examples, which were in a sense good practice for me in trying to apply CRT tenets to teacher practice specifically and to begin to articulate a racially conscious pedagogy more broadly. Furthermore, I began to see the potential for CRT as a dialogic practice in educational settings—that is to say that it is not only a theory that researchers can use to analyze teachers but is also one that can be used *with* teachers in order to come to new understandings of race together.

In Chapter 4, Elizabeth's motivation to challenge, even as a contrast to Sarah's to learn, was equally pedagogical. From my conversations with Elizabeth, I gained more insight into my personal ideas of what white educators need to do to combat our complicity in institutional racism. As we got into deep discussions about the definition of racism and the issue of blame, I learned what place responsibility plays in my understanding of how whites can overcome our complicity. While the issue of how to get whites to take on such responsibility (for racist outcomes in particular) is still in question, our conversations helped me better conceptualize, articulate, and even reform my own approach to racially conscious teacher education and research. I had learned how to *understand and express* CRT as a dialogical practice from Sarah, but with Elizabeth's great ability to question I had an opportunity to *engage in* CRT as dialogic practice.

Finally, in chapter 5, the dialogue with The Boys was the most atypical in comparison to that with the rest of the teachers. Yet, it perhaps gives some insight into how teacher educators can begin to promote racial responsibility. A combination of my own failure to analyze The Boys' thinking and the hope they were able to convey allowed for us to perform a dialogue of possibility. The fluidity of the conversation did allow me to see how racially conscious white teachers do try to challenge institutional racism in their practice by overcoming to some extent a reliance on built-in structures to fight racial disparity. A humanistic approach to education, the use of art and performance, and an articulation of personal experience as an outside perspective all arose as potentially antiracist practices, and they are all areas that can be further explored to understand more how they might help develop such practice. Even with the different nature of those interviews, by maintaining the same commitment to challenging institutional racism in schools I was able to tap into the performativity of conversations with white teachers about race. "As a communication practice, performing narrative makes conflict over experience, speaking and identify concrete and accessible" (Langellier and Peterson, 2004, p. 29). So, looking at John, Elijah, and David's conversations as performances of narrative, which are performed publicly, allowed me to focus on how these stories as "concrete and accessible" examples of challenges to institutional racism. In this sense the stories of John and Elijah in particular challenged the dominant institutional interpretations of race and racism in the school.

In general, from all the teachers I learned how to more fluently articulate a stance against colorblindness and the remnants of liberalism in educational settings and to more clearly explain critical understandings of race. I learned to use this language with the teachers in the study through critical engagement in the ideas from CRT, among other sources. Even though the interviews did build on each other and even though writing forces a certain linear presentation, this learning process of course was not so cleanly systematic. Writing in linear form does allow me to present a certain clarity of argument, but I think the reader can also pick apart my systemic presentation. I can imagine going back and forth between introduction and narrative chapter, between narrative chapter and conclusion, or between any combination of chapters. A clever reader could pick apart my arguments to point out incongruence, to find what epiphanies (i.e., "aha" moments) I may have missed, or (with some luck) to uncover some pedagogical moments that I may have created.

One particular area of critique that needs to be examined more closely is the influence of gender on my interviewing and analysis. In Chapter 5, I discuss the potentially different ways the women and men in this study articulated their adherence or resistance to liberalism and their approaches to antiracism. By not bracketing my interpretations of the difference in those articulations, I may have stated too strongly The Boys' success at critical antiracism and not strongly enough the women's. The end result is that I did not afford the women the same co-performer status as the men, and this may have affected how much I was able to learn from them. As I discussed in Chapter 5, I need to take the next step of analyzing gender, and in particular my gender privilege, along with race in my future work. So, since my intent was to position all the teachers as co-performers of the research act, I invite critique of my approach that might further highlight the antiracist commitments of the women in this study.

CRITICAL RACE THEORY AND SOCIOLOGY OF EDUCATION

Both CRT and the field of sociology of education have a history of analyzing and challenging racism. One of the similarities between CRT and the sociology of education is that both have been concerned with analyzing the construction and reconstruction of whiteness and white dominance. On its end, the sociology of education has been very useful in uncovering the links between white privilege and racism. For example, in the introduction I discussed the studies by Feagin and O'Brien (2003) and by Myers (2003) that analyze how whites talk about race and how such talk is connected to various forms of racism. While my study is similar to these in that it also is a study of whites talking about race, there are some key differences as well. Perhaps the most significant difference is in the research approach itself. Feagin and O'Brien (2003) investigate how whites in positions with a certain amount of power either adhere to or work against racist attitudes and practices. Their rationale is that these whites have a certain amount of influence the "social strata" and "social networks" (p. 28) which make up our society and thus uncovering their racial understandings is important to eventually work against racism. Myers (2003) similarly hopes to uncover how people, and not just whites, talk about race, especially in negative ways, which she calls racetalk. Her goal is to highlight such racetalk so as to show how it still exists in society, and that this illumination will help people challenge that practice.

My study has the similar objective of highlighting certain discourse with the hope that such exposure will help educators challenge it. However, drawing on the motivation of CRT to challenge racism and on Ladson-Billings' (1998) call to make this work relevant to teachers and students, I have attempted to use CRT to directly affect the practice of teachers in the study (enacting what Morrow [2000] would call a mediational study). Rather than only examine the phenomena of racetalk and extract information from my co-performers, I attempted to also challenge the colorblind and liberal views contained in such talk. Furthermore, I attempted to use the interview process as a learning tool, so I could better counter liberalism in the future. I do not at all mean to indicate that studies like Feagin and O'Brien's and Myers' are less useful than mine. In fact, they actually offer fuller descriptions of the complicated dynamics of racetalk. The scope of their studies exceeds mine in their examination of how whites talk about race and are especially useful in uncovering the key underlying ideologies that whites employ. Thus, those studies help me think about how to recognize and analyze the various forms of racetalk. The strength of my study, however, is that I do not only examine racetalk and its potentially negative consequences along with the liberal ideology that enables such talk to persist, but I also draw on Gallagher's (2000) caution about whites doing research on race with whites and attempt to challenge white racism as it emerges in the study.

Gallagher (2000) discusses how researchers can perpetuate inferential racism when they do research on race with whites because they may allow white participants to re-validate racist positions by eliciting comments that reveal such positions during the data collection process. So while Morrow (2000) may argue that not all social science research studies that adhere to critical theory need be of the participatory action model, failing to acknowledge how research on race may unintentionally support and even create space for reaffirmations of racist views and dispositions can actually counter some of the aims of critical research in sociology. In Chapter 1, I discussed how studies such as Jencks and Phillips (1998), Hallinan (1994), Kao, Tienda, & Schneider (1996), and Kalmijn and Kraaykamp (1996) run the risk of inadvertently supporting inferential racism because they do not take a critical stance on the interpretation of their data. Even the more critical qualitative studies that do more overtly challenge the perpetuation of racism such as Feagin and O'Brien's (2003) and Myers' (2003) can fall into the same trap in more subtle ways. If qualitative researchers rely only on other people using their findings to do the work of combating racism, they rely on an ethnographic textualism that falls into a liberal form of change. The assumption is that those findings will push the anti-racist agenda along (and they may indeed do so), but as they do not challenge the racism they encounter more directly in the context of the research act, they may also potentially perpetuate the adherence to problematic racial views of their participants. So while I agree with Morrow that not all studies of race in the sociology of education be participatory action research, I do make the recommendation that studies on race in the field—even those as insightful as those by Feagin and O'Brien and by Myers—examine more closely and highlight more explicitly their potential complicity in supporting inferential racism so that they may better adhere to their goal of actually challenging the perpetuation of racism. This is tricky of course. On one hand, we want to be able to draw out racist comments and thoughts so that they may be examined and also challenged. On the other, we do to not challenge to the point where our participants never share their thoughts on race for fear of being exposed or shut down in the research process. In my work, it has been CRT that has been valuable in my attempt to both uncover complicity in institutional racism and not reinscribe inferential racism.

As CRT has been central to my own ability to engage in a dialogic approach with the teachers I have worked with, it is important to clarify what it is about CRT that makes it effective in analyzing and challenging white racism in the research act and in helping teachers in particular to develop and articulate understandings of race and racism that challenge the dominant liberal ideology of schools. In Chapter 1, I explained three aspects in particular: the ability to name whiteness, the value of property analysis and the focus on revisioning accounts of racial disparity. I revisit each of those aspects here to discuss the implications for fields such as sociology of education that study race and racism in schools.

First, I have explained that naming whiteness involves highlighting the way in which systems of categorization are used to privilege white ways of being and seeing. Teachers can, for example, categorize a student's behavior according to a white norm of what is considered appropriate behavior. In chapter 2, Melissa describes how such a process occurs in schools when she discusses the behaviors teacher prefer to see from their students. However, teachers are not always so aware of how they categorize student behavior and it can be difficult to see how the process of categorization is racialized in a way that privileges whiteness. In chapter 4, my conversation with Elizabeth about how she characterized her Latino male students' behavior shows an example of how whiteness can be viewed and used as a labeling practice. She accurately named one student's behavior as inappropriate (sexually harassing another student), but when we discussed from where she derived her notion of appropriateness, she admitted that it was from a standard of whiteness, which she positioned at the top of a racial hierarchy of appropriate school behavior. She used one incident of one student to generalize the behavior of all her Latino male students according to a standard based on what she deemed to be a white way of being. Scholars of sociology of education of race can analyze the formation and employment of such hierarchal categorizations, specifically as they lead to daily schooling practices that reify white privilege.

Using the concept of whiteness as property (Harris 1995/1993) can deepen these analyses and help make the connection between those categorizations and their material effects on students of color. Scholars have shown how students of color (in particular black males) can be disciplined more harshly than white students for similar behaviors (Irvine, 1990; McCadden, 1998; Skiba, Michael, Nardo & Peterson, 2002; Monroe, 2005). By analyzing the systems of categorization that teachers use to make those decisions—such as how Elizabeth determines that her Latino male students are "aggressive"—scholars can engage teachers in discussions of how labeling practices can effect students of color differently from how they affect white students. This analysis need not be only of discipline practices. By analyzing how teachers base their judgments about which students are "good students" on standards of whiteness, scholars can highlight how teachers unintentionally affect their students' access to equitable curricula and instruction. For example, if schools privilege white forms of literacy, students of color can be labeled as less literate or remedial. Apple (2000) has described how the construction and legitimation of what is considered "official knowledge" can privilege students from privileged backgrounds. Scholars in sociology of education can use CRT to examine school practices rely exclusively on official knowledge—versus, for example, students' "funds of knowledge" (Moll, Amanti, Neff, and Gonzalez, 1992)—to regulate access to more rigorous and meaningful curriculum and instruction. Because CRT centers race in such analysis, scholars can examine specifically how the categorization of students can affect how teachers determine what types of books their students of color will read, what kinds of literacy activities they will engage in, and how central their background literacy experiences will be in the classroom. In this sense, scholars can analyze how the property of whiteness gives white students the right to use and enjoy literacy instruction that is central to the classroom experience while the teachers have the right to deny students of color the same privilege because of how they are labeled. In essence, the property of whiteness affects curriculum as a form property. Teachers' white ways of seeing prevent them from seeing students' non-white ways of being as valuable (i.e., they are not appropriate for school, they do not show the right kind of intelligence, etc.), so teachers deny students the same access to rigorous and meaningful curriculum.

Finally, CRT focuses not just on analyzing racial inequities in education but also on developing counternarratives that put these analyses in the context of the lives of real students and teachers. Researchers can attempt to disrupt categorization practices that are based in whiteness in the research act with their participants so as affect change in a more immediate sense. By focusing on systems of categorization and their relationship both to students' access to rigorous and meaningful curriculum and to schools' discipline practices, scholars can show that racial inequity need not be the result of overt racism but rather can occur despite teachers good intentions to be racially equitable. In this way, scholars can employ the practice of naming whiteness to show how teachers are complicit in institutional forms of racial inequity. In essence, teachers can learn a new story about the cause of racial disparity, a story that places them as actors and potential change agents.

An important aspect of developing counternarratives with teachers is to help teachers develop more critical understandings of race. This process includes a need to understand and counteract the limitations of liberal ideology. In this study, the critique of liberalism has been essential in the revisioning process. Prominent work in the field of sociology of education has analyzed the role of liberal ideology in perpetuating racial and other forms of inequity (see Apple, 2004; Giroux 2001, 1997; Torres, 1998; Omi and Winant, 1994 for just a few strong examples). In addition, McIntyre (1997) has undertaken similar work by focusing on racial consciousness raising with white pre-service teachers. What CRT offers to the critique of liberal ideology—through its analysis of systems of categorization and of whiteness and curriculum as property—is a way to show teachers how this critique is useful for them in pursuing racial equity because it helps teachers see how their own day-to-day words and actions support and sustain racial inequity. From a performance ethnography standpoint, this opens up the research act as being potentially transformative. "The danger of performing narrative is that by doing something in and with a discourse that is neither uniform nor stable, we risk changing the bodily practices and material conditions in which they are embedded: what is done can be undone" (Langellier and Peterson, 2004, p. 25). As I described above, naming the whiteness of how teachers categorize students and linking those categorizations to students' access (or lack of access)) to an equally rigorous and meaningful education can help teachers understand their complicity in racial disparity in a way that does not resort to labeling teachers as racist. Instead, it can help show teachers that un-critiqued criteria of what schools use to label students—e.g., "good student"—can lead teachers to unintentionally marginalize some students because of their race. Because it does not locate racism in the teachers themselves but rather in their complicity in wider institutional practices, CRT analysis can maintain the role of the teacher as potential resisters of institutionalized racial disparity. In that way, CRT analysis fits very well with a dialogic research approach.

In my professional experience, such a dialogic approach has been necessary to make the analyses offered by sociology of education useful to teachers. For the insights of sociology of education on race in particular to be useful, maintaining a commitment to the teachers I work with as allies is important. In research, positioning teachers as co-performers when conducting research helps maintain this commitment. At the same time, it is my job as a teacher educator (of social foundations and multicultural education, among other subjects) to challenge views that do not support equity in education. CRT analysis has helped me delve into challenging those views in teachers while still maintaining respect for the teachers as professionals that want to work towards against racism. This analysis uncovers the process of how white privilege and institutional racism are actively maintained through the actions of individual teachers. As Leonardo (2004) argues, when teaching whites about race we must move beyond discussions of white privilege as just something that whites possess and move towards analyses of how whites maintain that privilege. CRT offers me a way to examine specific examples of this process with teachers. By focusing on white privilege and institutional racism as processes that are still going on, two things can happen. One, teachers can let go of worrying about whether they are racist or not—it is not about static identity or labeling people but rather about how racist outcomes occur. Two, they can think about how to take part in counteracting the process. That is to say, they can think of ways to resist racially marginalizing practices.

I have found CRT's tenets and tools of analysis to be particularly engaging and useful for me in revisioning—again, *with* teachers—how institutional racism is formed and reified and in using this revisioning to move from liberal to critical understandings of race and racism. Sociology of education can achieve similar goals. Those researchers who have been part of the critical tradition in sociology of education have helped invaluable to me in developing a deeper understanding of institutional racism. As a teacher educator who uses the field to discuss race with my students, sociology has taught me how liberal ideology has sustained racial disparity in institutional ways. I hope my study has provided one example of how researchers on the sociology of race in education can continue to work from understandings of race and racism rooted in the critical tradition without using those understandings as normative stances (Morrow, 2000) that do not adequately capture the complex ways in which teachers and other social actors both support and resist institutional racism. By using the research act as a way to link individual practices to institutional structures, I hope to get closer analyzing racism in a way that balances structural explanation and individual meaning making. As Morrow states, *"the most fundamental dilemma of qualitative research in the problematic of analyzing social processes in terms of both structures and meanings"* (60–61, emphasis in the original). In other words, research that follows the vein of critical theory should not only pursue structural explanations of social phenomena, such as racial inequity in schools. Neither should it only pursue explanations of how social actors make meaning of those structures. Rather, research in the critical tradition works at analyzing the relationship between those two "explanatory strategies" (61) so as to come to better and *potentially emancipatory* understandings of social issues such as racial disparity. In the context of the study of race and racism in education, CRT can further an what Morrow calls an interpretive structural methodology because it can be used in a dialogic approach to inquiry that balances structure and meaning. Such a dialogic approach is key and actually a goal of research in critical theory.

DIALOGIC PERFORMANCE AS A BRIDGE

As Madison (2005) points out, performance ethnography is a critical approach to ethnography. As such, the ethnographer makes an attempt to affect the site in which he or she is conducting the research.

> Critical ethnography begins with an ethical responsibility to address processes of unfairness or injustice within a particular *lived* domain. By "ethical responsibility," I mean a compelling sense of duty and commitment based on moral principles of human freedom and well-being, and hence a compassion for suffering of living beings. The conditions for existence within a particular context are not as they *could* be for specific subjects; as a result, the researcher feels a moral obligation to make a contribution toward changing those conditions toward greater freedom and equity. The critical ethnographer also takes us beneath surface appearance, disrupts the *status quo*, and unsettles both neutrality and taken-for-granted assumptions by bringing to light underlying and obscure operations of power and control. (p. 5, all italics in original)

My study was an attempt to be critical in precisely these ways. The unfairness and injustice I see and am trying to affect in educational settings is racial disparity. Thus, I have a compassion for the students of color who I believe are suffering from the institutional forms of racism that still exist in schools. I believe that challenging white teachers on the negative aspects of colorblindness and liberalism that is part of their practice is, in effect, an effort to unsettle the neutrality and taken-for-granted-ness that such ideologies promote in order to uncover the obscured[1] forms of power that put students of color at a disadvantage.

At the same time, the performative nature of my research approach addresses the complex position in which teachers act. They are not merely power brokers in any traditional sense but more actors within a structure of schooling. As Melissa pointed out, unlike with some other types of jobs, teachers do not often intentionally put themselves in positions of power and they are not often seen as having much power. At the same time teachers do wield power, and they are certainly operating within larger power relationships. One of the prime ways a performance approach can balance these competing roles is by positioning teachers as co-performers in educational research. In this position, then, researchers and teachers together can come to understand the dynamics of power and can together imagine the possibilities for challenging that power. Situating teachers as co-performers is an important practice because, to paraphrase Madison (2005), as educational researchers we cannot assume that teachers do not already attempt to challenge power and that they do not already do so in ways we cannot see because of our own different professional and epistemological contexts.

Dialogical performance has been particularly important in my use of performance ethnography precisely because it both acknowledges the power of the researched and maintains a critical stance. As I stated in the introduction, dialogic performance encourages the researchers and the researched to challenge each other so as they may both learn from each other. For the researched to be able to challenge the researcher, their points of view must be considered valid. At the same time, the researcher can avoid romanticizing the participant's point of view and can maintain his or her own. When each point of view has equal weight and by bringing these points of view into dialogue with each other, the performance researcher allows the fissures in the ideologies that support those points of view to show. In this study,

I hoped that the dialogue with teachers would help illuminate the fissures in colorblindness and liberalism. These ideologies employ means of signification and categorization, what Conquergood (1998) calls symbols, that I believe mask the nature of racism in school settings. So, I hoped that I was able to expose those symbols so that the teachers could see how they actually interfere with the other (more positive aspects) of their own racial ideologies.

Since dialogical performance offers a way to analyze symbols, as a practice it resonates well with one of the core ideas of CRT. As Delgado and Stefancic (2000) have argued, white dominance is maintained when whites adhere to certain systems of categorization. Similarly Conquergood (1998) describes the importance of symbols in cultural politics.

> Symbols instill belief and shape attitudes that underpin social structures. The binding force of culture, by and large, is a web of symbols that enables people to control and make sense out of experience in patterned ways. (Conquergood, 1998, p. 11)

In this study I have argued that such webs of symbols include how teachers classify students as good students or not and how teachers adhere to only possibilities to racial change that rely on current institutional structures. Racial disparity is one of the results of the patterned ways that then develop from how teachers use these symbols. The process of give and take with teachers positioned as intellectual equals that is involved a dialogical approach allows these patterns to be exposed.

The process of challenging each other, of delving into each other's thought processes and logics, and of analyzing specific instances of racial disparity allowed me to address the existence of racism on schools in a deeper way than I can normally with pre-service teachers. I did not always move these teachers as much as I would have liked or in exactly the way I would have liked but I did learn a great deal about the complexity of teachers' conceptualizations of colorblindness—the ways in which they both connect to and veer away from liberalism, for example—and how white teachers can break away from an uncritical adherence to colorblindness.

> The oft quoted phrase "Knowledge is power" reflects how narrow perception, limited modes of understanding, and uncritical thinking diminish the capacity to envision alternative life possibilities; domestication will prohibit new forms of addressing conflict, and it will dishonor the foreign and the different. Knowledge is power relative to social justice, because knowledge guides and equips us to identify, name, question, and act against the unjust; consequently we unsettle another layer of complicity. (Madison, 2005, pp. 5–6)

I hope the dialogue I had with the teachers in this study helped them develop an ability to identify and name symbols, categorizations, and practices that reinscribe racial disparity. I also hope it is educative for us in teacher education to imagine how to unsettle all layers and modes of complicity.

In the end, dialogical performance is an approach that can employ the critical stances of traditions such as CRT, critical theory, feminism, etc. in order to better work towards the goals of those traditions. In this vein, dialogical performance is an extension of those traditions, a way to bring critique to new spaces. For me using CRT in a dialogic performance approach allowed me to bridge the field of sociology of education with the world of practicing teachers. It has enabled me to bring the theoretical insights I have gained about race and racism and to ground them in the thoughts and lives of teachers. Furthermore, it has also enabled me to use sociology of education in a way that makes its politics on race explicit. This has been an overt attempt to address what for me has been two of the shortcomings of the field of sociology of education with regards to race research: 1) its adherence to traditional positioning of research subjects, and 2) its tendency to assume that research will affect the lives of students of color without specifically and actively being highly attuned to how the research act can achieve such transformative goals. These shortcomings are related to the field's over-reliance on the ethnographic textualism that I discuss in chapter 1. Therefore, rather than only analyze the teachers' thoughts and actions according to the tenets of CRT, I attempted to communicate CRT's modes of analysis to the teachers so we both could understand the potential consequences of thoughts and actions regarding race. Similarly, rather than only focus on how this study will inform those who read about it (via this book, journal articles, etc.), I explicitly intended to use this research to help the teachers in the study better realize racial equity as well as to help me better work toward the same goal in my work as a teacher educator. By having the teachers take part in the process of analysis, I hope they have become able to use CRT as part of their praxis, a hope I have for myself as well.

Using CRT in this give-and-take way with teachers, then, has been an attempt for me to create a common language for the conversation on race. One of the goals has been to promote critical reflection with these teachers and to devise a way to promote a mode of critical reflection on race that can be used in teacher education. In that sense dialogic performance is a bridge that can enable two different spaces (with two different ideological biases and two different lexicons) to meet and learn from each other. For me, dialogical performance has been a bridge between theoretical understandings of race in education and the thinking of teachers, and this bridge enables me to conduct "a sustained analysis of performing narrative" (Langellier and Peterson, 2004, p. 30). The conversations that result from interviewing are not only data that I put theory to but are also performances themselves, performances that shape the way the teachers and I understand both racial theory and actual racialized experiences. Focusing on research as performing narrative allowed me to be acutely aware not only of how the teachers both sustained and resisted liberal forms of racism but also of how my research both sustains and resists traditional and liberal understandings of research on race. I discuss this tension in the next section.

CONTRADICTION, CLARITY, AND COMMITTING

In a study that critiques liberalism in schools and educational research, I have also supported that same liberalism, in part because of my belief that the type of research I propose will bring about progress towards racial equity. The idea of progress is a problematic one if it is not contested and contextualized. Progress in specific, current material conditions is something to work for in the sense that those conditions can be affected so that some people will no longer continue to suffer as much from practices such as institutional racism. The idea of progress—articulated in this context-specific manner—does not necessarily counter the critical epistemology of CRT. However, if in the context of this study I have envisioned progress towards the elimination of racism as easily achievable via research in schools (evening if it is in the most dialogic manner), I fall into the same liberal trap of believing that major change in racial disparity in schools can come without a radical shift in the institution of schooling. Despite the critical analysis I may have been able to promote, it would be hard for me to argue that I caused such a radical shift in the schools where these teachers worked. It is in this way, oddly enough, that my claims of what has been achieved in this study are linked at least partially to liberal ideology. By pursing antiracism with the teachers in this study specifically and in the field of teacher education more broadly, I adhere to the assumption that the educational system can provide emancipation from racial oppression. Liberal ideology promotes change via the structures embedded in societal structures. Following that ideology, I have laid at least part of my faith in transformation the current structure(s) of schooling, the very same system I critique.

In addition, there is a white privilege to my claims about the work I have done towards the goals of antiracism. Without having to understand or feel first hand the effects of racism, and without having talked to any students of color about how these white teachers have affected them in the context of this study, I have made claims that at least some progress towards antiracism has been made. I can throw myself into the mix of critical race scholars and be the "cool white man studying race" while also enjoying the benefits that engaging in this scholarship can bring me (e.g., merit towards tenure). I can do all of this while reinscribing a liberal idea of the value of educational research. So, my performance as education researcher/race-worker contains at least the same level of contradiction as the teachers' performances as socially just educators. That is a contradiction I will have to sit with until either I can formulate a way to either get away from progress as located in school sites or until I do more work to show how this type of inquiry does, indeed, affect material consequences in a substantive way. In the meantime, I hope I can also work against my complicity in the reification of liberalism by maintaining a commitment to agenda and epistemology of critical race theory.

Drawing on Noblit's (1999) work, I have in my own work discussed the importance of committing when whites do work on race (Blaisdell, 2005). Noblit explains the importance of ethnographers to commit to the people they are working with and to the knowledge project they are working within. To make their work ethical, researchers commit to people, and they commit to understanding. As researchers, our own perspectives color how we interpret what we see and here. Therefore, committing to the people with whom we research (i.e., the "participants," to use more traditional language) can help us honor their intentions. Committing to understanding their point of view as much as possible helps us keep our own understandings in check. "If we do not work against ourselves, work against our values and identities, then they always get in the way of our understanding someone else's point of view" (Noblit, 1999, p. 7). Therefore, I add that this committing—which Noblit contends must remain a verb so as to emphasize its ongoing, never-completed nature—involves sitting in an ambiguous situation when whites do work on race. Whites have a racial privilege that we always carry with us, so we must be careful not to only be ventriloquists for people of color (Gómez-Peña, 1996), in effect stealing other people's words and ideas and claiming them to be our own. Much of what has been discussed about race by whites has already been understood and articulated by scholars of color. So, when whites do race work we must continually commit to the people that have had these understandings and articulated them before us.

In working within a field such as CRT, this committing is especially important, as it is a theory that originates from scholars of color and a perspective that scholars from "the bottom" (to use Matsuda's 1995/1987 term) can have a special understanding of. It is an ethically ambiguous practice for me to use CRT. On the one hand, I hope that it has enabled me to work against racism in the context if teacher education. On the other, in centering CRT in my work I promote myself as an "expert" in the field and somewhat ignore the recommendation to let scholars of color take the forefront in this work. I hope that by committing, I at least mitigate the negative effects of such an appropriation.

So, in this study I have attempted to use CRT in a way that honors its commitment to racial change. By taking it to the context of schools, I have tried to use the theory in a field where I believe whites can operate to work towards that racial change. What is still important in this agenda, however, is that I do not merely use CRT as a simple means of one-time analysis. To do so would be to miss the epistemological implications of critical race studies. Bell (1995/1976) and Delgado (1995/1984) have pointed out the conflict in agenda that can exist between scholars and activists because of their different contexts and backgrounds. Therefore, in order to uphold CRT's antiracist agenda in my work as a researcher and teacher educator, I must continue to work towards understanding the theory better and draw from the wisdom of critical race scholars. Among other things, this means I must understand my own privilege and check my own complicity in institutional racism. Rather than believe that I have the answer to how whites can use CRT in practice, I must invite critique of my work from scholars of color, among other scholars who have connections to marginalized groups. I can put my work out in the discourse on race in education but must check my assertions with the understandings of colleagues that have experiences and perspectives different from my own. In this way, I hope I can continue to engage in critical race theory and practice so as to work towards racial equity at least in some small way.

To honor this same committing, scholars can work in areas not addressed by this study. I have attempted to address some of the ways in which liberalism negatively affects the thought and practice of teachers. Through modes such labeling students and adhering to existing structures of potential change, teachers can limit the access to curriculum for the students of color. There are also many aspects of liberalism I did not address. For example, I did not talk to the students that these teachers work with. I am sure that their voices, understandings, and wisdom would call for a complicated re-working of my articulation of potential racial change. Likewise, as parents are discussed by some of the teachers, those parents' perspectives would be an important component of constructing antiracist practice. From a theoretical standpoint, there are many perspectives I also leave out or only address in a rudimentary way. One of these is of course a gender studies standpoint. While I briefly discuss the possible differences between the men and women in this study, a more thorough analysis would offer insight into the many interrelated causes inequity in schools and how teachers can and do address that inequity.

Perhaps one of the most pedagogical aspects of this study for me is that it has helped me begin to develop language that I can use with in- and pre-service teachers to discuss the phenomenon of racism in schools with without instilling senses of guilt or blame. This language development is important as language—especially as it is linked to our systems of classification—affects our ways of being (Delgado and Stefancic, 2000; Madison, 2005). The language whites use to describe issues of race and racism can link us to ideologies that make us complicit in institutional forms of oppression. Therefore, being able to use a language with white pre- and in-service teachers that highlights that complicity without prompting those teachers to retreat from the conversation is an important step. However, as I said above, I have *started* to develop this language, and the analytical tools of CRT have helped me enter these conversations. I have not yet used this language in practice extensively. I have tied to use it with the teachers in this study and in the college courses I have taught. A more thorough investigation of how this language could work in a myriad of contexts would prove its potential benefits and help develop the contextual nuances that prevent and promote its development. Simply put, this language has to be put into practice to see if it does, indeed, lead to material changes.

Another powerful lesson of this study for me is that it has been a means for me to learn how to use methods as a researcher, formulate a theoretical framework for my work, and position myself as a new scholar. It has also helped me pursue an agenda for my career as an educational researcher and teacher educator that is highly personal. In that way, the dialogic performance approach of this study has been another type of bridge for me. It has enabled me to connect academic analysis with more performative, embodied modes of inquiry. Urrieta (2003) discussed the dissonance between personal experience and the academic voice. He claimed that academic prose can make invisible, mask, and discount very important aspects of personal experience that actually support and make stronger our academic work. Some of the work academics do, such as the fight against racism, is highly personal. For me, CRT in dialogic performance has allowed me to bridge an academic mode of inquiry with a personal one. Specifically, it has helped me, to borrow John's phrase, "see with poetic eyes" the complexities and contradictions of race work. In addition to giving me an academically theoretical way to examine and challenge racism, the approach I took in this study allowed me to see the wisdom contained in the teachers' thoughts and words. At times, these thoughts and words were often astute analyses of the complex existence of racism in schools. As such, they taught me how to better analyze that racism. At other times, those thoughts and words contained knowledge about how to combat racism, knowledge I did not have until I spoke with these teachers. This process has been, for me, truly dialogic.

This book is based on my dissertation work and, in essence, the dissertation is itself a performance. It is performative (i.e., I perform myself as educational researcher, showing publicly that I have earned the credentials I receive) and pedagogical (i.e., I learn some of the methods and theory necessary to be that educational researcher). Laying my performance out in writing is an opportunity for it to be analyzed for its pedagogical potential with regard to antiracist teacher and researcher practice. As I reflect back on this performance, key phrases stand out for me. Seeing every student as a ten. Being an equal opportunity pusher. Wanting to move heart. Seeing with poetic eyes. These phrases stand out for both their simplicity and their complexity. In each of those phrases lies an epistemological standpoint that can mask a teacher's complicity in racism. Yet, in each also lies the possibility to engage teachers in the development of antiracist practice. Even though the teachers in this study lay at different places along the racially conscious spectrum, these phrases indicate to me that many white teachers already carry with them the seeds to enact racially conscious practice. They indicate that while white teachers may still adhere to liberalism in the way they envision the achievement of racial equity, they simultaneously carry motivations that may resist that liberalism. Thus they already have their own levels of committing that scholars of education can draw upon. It is the committing of teachers to racial change that helps give me the motivation to stick with the field of teacher education as a sight for potential social justice, and the "what could be" that the fight against racism may bring

NOTES

1 Note, I think using the verb form (and not the adjective) is important because it emphasizes that power is not inherently obscure but hidden by actors, ideologies, and practices.

REFERENCES

Aaronson, J. U. (1999). Recruiting, supporting, and retaining new teachers: A retrospective look at programs in the District of Columbia public schools. *The Journal of Negro Education, 68*, 335–342.

Allen, J., & Hermann-Wilmarth, J. (2004). Cultural construction zones. *Journal of Teacher Education, 55*(3), 214–226.

Apple, M. W. (2000). *Official knowledge: Democratic education in a conservative age.* New York: Routledge.

Apple, M. W. (2004). *Ideology and curriculum.* New York: RoutledgeFalmer.

Ballantine, J. H. (2001). *The sociology of education.* Upper Saddle River, NJ: Prentice Hall.

Banks, J. A. (Ed.). (1995). *Handbook of research on multicultural education.* New York: MacMillan.

Bell, D. A. (1995). Serving two masters: integration ideals and client interests in school desegregation litigation. In K. W. Crenshaw, N. Gotanda, G. Peller, & K. Thomas (Eds.), *Critical race theory: Key writings that defined the movement* (pp. 5–19). New York: New Press. (Originally in *Yale Law Journal, 85*, 470–478. (1976)).

Bell, D. A. (1995). Brown V. Board of Education and the interest convergence dilemma. In K. W. Crenshaw, N. Gotanda, G. Peller, & K. Thomas (Eds.), *Critical race theory: Key writings that defined the movement* (pp. 20–29). New York: New Press. (Originally in *Harvard Law Review, 93*(3), 518–533. (Jan. 1980)).

Blaisdell, B. (2005). Seeing every student as a 10: Using critical race theory to engage white teachers' colorblindness. *International Journal of Educational Policy, Research, and Practice, 6*(1), 3–22.

Blaisdell, B. (2005). Sitting with ourselves: How to work against white guilt in anti-racist teacher education. In S. Hughes (Ed.), *What we still don't know about race: How to talk about it in the classroom.* Lewiston, NY: Mellen Press.

Boal, A. (1985/1979). *Theatre of the oppressed.* New York: Theatre Communications Group.

Boal, A. (1995). *The rainbow of desire: The Boal method of theatre and therapy* (A. Boal, Trans.). New York: Routledge.

Boal, A. (1995). *Games for actors and non-actors* (A. Jackson, Trans.). New York: Routledge.

Cochran-Smith, M. (1995). Color blindness and basket making are not the answers: Confronting the dilemmas of race, culture, and language diversity in teacher education. *American Educational Research Journal, 32*(3), 493–522.

Cohen, J. (1993). Constructing race at an urban high school: In their minds, their mouths their hearts. In L. Weis & M. Fine (Eds.), *Beyond silenced voices: Class, race, and gender in United States schools* (pp. 289–308). Albany, NY: SUNY.

Connell, R. W. (1987). *Gender and power.* Stanford, CA: Stanford University Press.

Conquergood, D. (1985). Performing as a moral act: Ethical dimensions of the ethnography of performance. *Literature in Performance, 5*, 1–13.

Conquergood, D. (1991). Rethinking ethnography: Towards a critical cultural politics. *Communication Monographs, 58*, 179–194.

Conquergood, D. (1998). Beyond the text: Toward a performative cultural politics. In S. J. Dailey (Ed.), *The future of performance studies: Visions and revisions* (pp. 25–36). Washington: National Communication Association.

Dale, R. (1976). *Schooling and capitalism: A sociological reader.* London: Routledge & Kegan Paul, in association with The Open University Press.

Davis, P. (1989). Law as microaggression. *Yale Law Journal, 98*, 1559–1577.

Delgado, R. (1995). The imperial scholar: Reflections on a review of civil rights literature. In K. W. Crenshaw, N. Gotanda, G. Peller, & K. Thomas (Eds.), *Critical race theory: Key writings that defined the movement* (pp. 46–57). New York: New Press. (Originally in *University of Pennsylvania Law Review, 132*(3), 561–578. (March 1984)).

Delgado, R., & Stefancic, J. (1992). The imperial scholar revisited: How to marginalize outsider writing, ten years later. *University of Pennsylvania Law Review, 140*, 1349–1372.

Delgado, R., & Stefancic, J. (2000). *Critical race theory: the cutting edge.* Philadelphia: Temple University.

Delgado, R., & Stefancic, J. (2001). *Critical race theory: An introduction.* New York: New York University.

Delpit, L. (1995). Other people's children: Cultural conflict in the classroom. New York: New Press.

Denzin, N.K. (2003). *Performance ethnography*. Thousand Oaks, CA: Sage.
Denzin, N. K., & Lincoln, Y. S. (1994). *Handbook of qualitative research*. Thousand Oaks, CA: Sage Publications.
DuBois, W. E. B. (1903). *The souls of black folk essays and sketches*. Chicago: A. C. McClurg & Co.
DuBois, W. E. B. (1935). Does the Negro need separate schools? *Journal of Negro Education, 4*(3), 328–335.
Duncan, G. A. (2004). *Schooling and inequality in post-industrial America: Toward a critical ethnography of time*. Paper presented at the American Educational Research Association annual meeting, San Diego, CA, April 12–16.
Feagin, J., & O'Brien, E. (2003). *White men on race: Power, privilege, and the shaping of cultural consciousness*. Boston: Beacon.
Fischer, C. S., Hout, M., Jaankowski, M. S., Lucas, S. R., Swidler, A., & Voss. K. (1996). *Inequality by design: cracking the bell curve myth*. Princeton, NJ: Princeton University Press.
Foster, M. (1993). Resisting racism: Personal testimonies of African-American teachers. In L. Weis & M. Fine (Eds.), *Beyond silenced voices: Class, race, and gender in United States schools* (pp. 273–288). Albany, NY: SUNY.
Frankenberg, R. (1993). *White women, race matters: the social construction of whiteness*. Minneapolis, MN: University of Minnesota.
Freeman, A. (1990). Antidiscrimination law: The view from 1989. *Tulane Law Review, 64*.
Fuoss, K. (1997). *Striking performances/performing strikes*. Jackson, MS: University Press of Mississippi.
Gallagher, M. (2000). White like me?: Methods, meaning and manipulation in the field of white studies. In F. Winddance Twine & J. Warren (Eds.), *Race-ing research, researching race: Methodological and ethical dilemmas in field research* (pp. 67–92). New York: New York University.
Gilligan, C. (1982). *In a different voice: Psychological theory and women's development*. Cambridge, MA: Harvard University Press.
Giroux, H. A. (2001). *Theory and resistance in education: Towards a pedagogy for the opposition, revised and expanded edition*. Westport, CT: Berginand Garvey.
Giroux, H. A. (1997). Pedagogy and the politics of hope: Theory, culture, and schooling: A critical reader. *The edge, critical studies in educational theory*. Boulder, CO: Westview Press.
Gómez-Peña, G. (1996). *The new world border: prophecies, poems, and loqueras for the end of the century*. San Francisco: City Lights.
Guinier, L., & Torres, G. (2002). *The miner's canary: Enlisting race, resisting power, transforming democracy*. Cambridge, MA: Harvard University.
Hall, S. (1981). The whites of their eyes: Racist ideologies and the media. In G. Bridges & R. Brunt (Eds.), *Silver linings: Some strategies for the eighties*. London: Lawrence and Wishart.
Hall, S. (1997). *Representation: Cultural representations and signifying practices*. London; Thousand Oaks, CA: Sage.
Harris, C. I. (1995). Whiteness as property. In K. W. Crenshaw, N. Gotanda, G. Peller, & K. Thomas (Eds.), *Critical race theory: Key writings that defined the movement* (pp. 276–291). New York: New Press. (Originally in *Harvard Law Review, 106*(8), 1709–1791. (June 1993)).
Henze, R., Lucas, T., & Scott, B. (1998). Dancing with the monster: Teachers discuss racism, power, and white privilege in education. *Urban Review, 30*(3), 187–210.
Hytten, K., & Warren, J. (2003). Engaging whiteness: How racial power gets reified in education. *Qualitative Studies in Education, 16*(1), 65–89.
Iglesias, E. M. (2002). Global markets, racial spaces, and the role of critical race theory in the struggle for community control of investments: And institutional class analysis. In F. Valdes, J. McCristal Culp, & A. P. Harris (Eds.), *Crossroads, directions, and a new critical race theory* (pp. 310–336). Philadelphia: Temple University.
Irvine, J. J. 1990. *Black students and school failure: Policies, practices, and prescriptions*. New York: Praeger.
Johnson, L. (2002). My eyes have been opened: White teachers and racial awareness. *Journal of Teacher Education, 53*(2), 153–167.
Kailin, J. (1999). How white teachers perceive the problem of racism in their schools: A case study in "liberal" lakeview. *Teachers College Record, 100*(4), 724–750.
Kincheloe, J. L., & Steinberg, S. R. (1998). Addressing the crisis of whiteness: Reconfiguring white identity in a pedagogy of whiteness. In J. L. Kincheloe, S. R. Steinberg, N. M. Rodriguez, & R. E. Chennault (Eds.), *White reign: Deploying whiteness in America* (pp. 3–29). New York: St. Martin's Press.

Laosa, L. (2001). The new segregation. *Policy Notes, 10*(1), 1–11.

Ladson-Billings, G. (1995). But that's just good teaching! The case for culturally relevant pedagogy. *Theory into Practice, 34*(3), 159.

Ladson-Billings, G. (1998). Just what is critical race theory and what's it doing in a nice field like education. *Qualitative Studies in Education, 11*(1), 7–24.

Ladson-Billings, G., & Tate, W. F. (1995). Toward a critical race theory of education. *Teachers College Record, 97*(1), 47–68.

Langellier, K., & Peterson, E. E. (2004). *Storytelling in daily life: Performing narrative.* Philadelphia: Temple University Press.

Lawrence, S. M., & Tatum, B. D. (1997). Teachers in transition: The impact of antiracist professional development on classroom practice. *Teachers College Record, 99*(1), 62–78.

Lazos Vargas, S. R. (2003). Introduction: Critical race theory in education: Theory, practice, and recommendations. In G. R. Lopez & L. Parker (Eds.), *Interrogating racism in qualitative research methodology* (pp. 1–18). New York: Peter Lang.

Leonardo, Z. (2004). The color of supremacy: Beyond the discourse of 'white privilege.' *Educational Philosophy and Theory, 36*(2), 137–152.

Lynn, M., & Parker, L. (2006). Critical race studies in education: Examining a decade of research on U.S. schools. *The Urban Review, 38*(4), 257–290.

Lyons, N. P. (1988). Two perspectives: On self, relationships, and morality. In C. Gilligan, J. V. Ward, J. M. Taylor, & B. Bardige (Eds.), *Mapping the moral domain: A contribution of women's thinking to psychological theory and education* (pp. 21–48). Cambridge, MA: Harvard.

Madison, D. S. (2005). *Critical ethnography: method, ethics, and performance.* Thousand Oaks, CA: Sage.

Marx, S., & Pennington, J. (2003). Pedagogies of critical race theory: Experimentation with white preservice teachers. *Qualitative Studies in Education, 16*(1), 91–110.

Matsuda, M. J. (1991). Voices of America: Accent, antidiscrimination law, and a jurisprudence for the last reconstruction. *Yale Law Journal, 100*(5), 1329–1407.

Matsuda, M. J. (1995). Looking to the bottom: Critical legal studies and reparations. In K. W. Crenshaw, N. Gotanda, G. Peller, K. Thomas (Eds.), *Critical race theory: Key writings that defined the movement* (pp. 63–79). New York: New Press. (Originally in *Harvard Civil Rights-Civil Liberties Law Review, 22*(2), 323–399. (Spring 1987)).

Matsuda, M., Lawrence, C., Delgado, R., & Crenshaw, K. (1993). *Words that wound: Critical race theory, assaultive speech, and the first amendment.* Boulder, CO: Westview Press.

McCadden, B. M. (1998). Why is Michael always getting timed out? Race, class, and the disciplining of other people's children. In R. E. Butchart & B. McEwan (Eds.), *Classroom discipline in American schools problems and possibilities for democratic education.* Albany, NY: State University of New York Press.

McCarthy, C. (2003). Contradictions of power and identity: Whiteness studies and the call of teacher education. *Qualitative Studies in Education, 16*(1) 127–133.

McIntyre, A. (1997). Constructing an image of a white teacher. *Teachers College Record, 98*(4), 653–681.

McNamee, S. J., & Miller, R. K. (2004). *The meritocracy myth.* Lanham, MD: Rowman & Littlefield.

Merseth, Mont, D., & Rees, D. I. (1996). The influence of classroom characteristics on high school teacher turnover. *Economic Inquiry, 34*, 152–167.

Metz, M. H. (1990). How social class differences shape teachers' work. In M. W. McLaughlin, J. E. Talbert, & N. Bascia (Eds.), *The contexts of teaching in secondary schools: Teachers' realities* (pp. 40–107). New York: Teachers College.

Moll, L. C., Amanti, C., Neff, D., & Gonzalez, N. (1992). Funds of knowledge for teaching: Using a qualitative approach to connect homes and classrooms. *Theory into Practice, 31*(1), 132–141.

Monroe, C. R. (2005). Why are "bad boys" always black? Causes of disproportionality in school discipline and recommendations for change. *Clearing House: A Journal of Educational Strategies, Issues and Ideas, 79*(1), 45–50.

Morrow, R. (2000). Social theory and educational research: Reframing the quantitative-qualitative distinction through a critical theory of methodology. In K. A. McClafferty, C. A, Torres, & T. R. Mitchell (Eds.), *Challenges of urban education: Sociological perspectives for the next century* (pp. 47–77). Albany, NY: State University of New York.

Murillo, E. G., Jr. (1999). Mojado crossings along neoliberal borderlands. *Educational Foundations, 13*(1), 7–30.

Myers, K. A. (2005). *Racetalk: Racism hiding in plain sight.* Lanham, MD: Rowman and Littlefield.
Noblit, G. W. (1999). *Particularities: Collected essays on ethnography and education.* New York: Lang.
Noblit, G. W., Flores, S., & Murillo, E. G., Jr. (2004). *Postcritical ethnography: Reinscribing critique.* Cresskill, NJ: Hampton.
Noddings, N. (1992). *The challenge to care in schools: an alternative approach to education.* New York: Teachers College.
Oakes, J., Wells, A. S., Jones, M., & Datnow, A. (1997). Detracking: The social construction of ability, cultural politics, and resistance to reform. *Teachers College Record, 98*, 482–510.
Omi, M., & Winant, H. (1994). Racial formation in the United States: From the 1960s to the 1990s. New York: Routledge.
Omi, M., & Winant, H. (1993). On the theoretical concept of race. In C. McCarthy & W. Crichlow (Eds.), *Race, identity and representation in education* (pp. 3–10). New York: Routledge.
Parker, L. (1998). "Race is…race aint": An exploration of the utility of critical race theory in qualitative research in education. *Qualitative Studies in Education, 11*(1), 43–55.
Pierce, C., Carew, J., Pierce-Gonzalez, D., & Willis, D. (1978). An experiment in racism: TV commercials. In C. Pierce (Ed.), *Television and education* (pp. 62–88). Beverly Hills, CA: Sage.
Popkewitz, T. S. (1998). The sociology of knowledge and the sociology of education: Michel Foucault and critical traditions. In C. A. Torres & T. R. Mitchell (Eds.), *Sociology of education emerging perspectives.* Albany, NY: State University of New York.
Rodriguez, N. M. (2000). Projects of whiteness in a critical Pedagogy. In N. M. Rodriguez & L. E. Villaverde (Eds.), *Dismantling white privilege: Pedagogy, politics, and whiteness* (pp. 1–24). New York: Peter Lang.
Skiba, R. J., Michael, R. S., Nardo, A. C., & Peterson, R. L. (2002). The color of discipline sources of racial and gender disproportionality in school punishment. *Urban Review, 34*(4), 317–342.
Sleeter, C. E. (1992). *Keepers of the American dream: A study of staff development and multicultural education.* Washington, DC: Falmer.
Sleeter, C. E. (1993). How white teachers construct race. In C. McCarthy & W. Crinchlow (Eds.), *Race, identity, and representation in education* (pp. 157–171). New York: Routledge.
Sleeter, C. (2001). Preparing teachers for culturally diverse schools: Research and the overwhelming presence of whiteness. *Journal of Teacher Education, 52*(2), 94–106.
Solórzano, D., Ceja, M., & Yosso, T. (2000). Critical race theory, racial microaggressions, and campus racial climate: The experiences of African American college students. *Journal of Negro Education, 69*(1–2), 60–73.
Solórzano, D. G., & Delgado Bernal, D. (2001). Examining transformational resistance through a critical race and Latcrit theory framework: Chicana and Chicano students in an urban context. *Urban Education, 36*(3), 308–342.
Steele, C. (1997). Threat in the air: How stereotypes shape intellectual identity and performance. *American Psychologist, 52*(6), 613–629.
Tatum, B. D. (1997). *"Why are all the black kids sitting together in the cafeteria?" and other conversations about race.* New York: Basic Books.
Thompson, A. (2003). Tiffany, friend of people of color: White investments in antiracism. *Qualitative Studies in Education, 16*(1), 7–29.
Thompson, J. B. (1990). *Ideology and modern culture: Critical social theory and in the era of mass communications.* Stanford, CA: Stanford University.
Torres, C. A. (1998). *Democracy, education, and multiculturalism: Dilemmas of citizenship in global world.* Lanham, MD: Rowman & Littlefield.
Urrieta, L. (2007). Community commitment and activist scholarship. *Journal of Hispanic Higher Education, 6*(3), 222–236.
Urrieta, L. (2003). Las identidades también lloran: Exploring the human side of indigenous Latina/o identities. *Educational Studies, 34*(2), 147–168.
Valenzuela, A. (1999). *Subtractive schooling U.S.-Mexican youth and the politics of caring.* Albany, NY: State University of New York Press.
Villenas, S. (1996). The colonizer/colonized Chicana ethnographer: Identity, marginalization, and co-optation in the field. *Harvard Educational Review*, 66(4), 711–731.

www.ingramcontent.com/pod-product-compliance
Lightning Source LLC
LaVergne TN
LVHW010611110826
845149LV00003B/869